FIRST WORLD WAR POEMS

FIRST WORLD WAR
POEMS

edited by ANDREW MOTION

faber and faber

First published in 2003
by Faber and Faber Limited
3 Queen Square London WC1N 3AU

Photoset by Wilmaset Ltd, Birkenhead, Wirral
Printed in England by
T. J. International Ltd, Padstow, Cornwall

Selection and introduction © Andrew Motion, 2003

The right of Andrew Motion to be identified as author
of this work has been asserted in accordance with Section 77
of the Copyright, Designs and Patents Act 1988

A CIP record for this book
is available from the British Library

ISBN 0-571-21207-7

2 4 6 8 10 9 7 5 3 1

Contents

Introduction

It's easy and difficult to make an anthology of First World War poetry. Easy because the best poems are well-known, and difficult for the same reason: what new is there to show? No other body of writing was revered in the same way in Britain during the twentieth century, and few authors had reputations like Wilfred Owen, Siegfried Sassoon and the rest. It wasn't just the quality of their work which made them special, it was the fact they had been there – fought, suffered and in many cases died. Their value as witnesses ('all a poet can do today is warn', Owen famously said) became inseparable from their role as makers. And even though the war they endured was in many respects unique, it became archetypal in their account. Not so much the war to end all wars (which anyway ended none and started a few), as the war to show the horror of all wars. That's why even the strongest poet of the Second World War – Keith Douglas – struggles to find anything like the same size of readership. To many people he seems less of a war poet because he's a different sort of war poet.

In the early years of a new century, things seem unlikely to change. Poetry of the First World War is still a part of the staple diet in our schools, which means it's still dripped into the national bloodstream at a steady rate. Its status as a sacred national text is confirmed every year on and around Armistice Day. And there is no reason to regret this – no reason to think the poems aren't worth studying, or to doubt their value as commemoration and admonition. But there's a problem, all the same. The poems risk becoming less and less intimate *as poems*, as they are more and more widely accepted as state furniture. Their fame makes them glassy, so we slip off their surfaces when we want to penetrate their depths. What is indispensable about them can also make them seem ossified.

That's why a new anthology is necessary. To re-present the poems as living things – often magnificent, sometimes flawed, occasionally short-sighted, and always human. Of course there are some familiar aspects to this book: its chronological structure, for one thing, which runs from Thomas Hardy's sombre warnings, to Rupert Brooke's more optimistic jingoism, to the quickly-deteriorating terrain of northern France, then beyond. (Brooke gets a lot of stick these days for his sonnets of 1914, and it's easy to see why: they're self-aggrandising, and fatally unimaginative about the reality of war. But their weaknesses have the value and interest of being typical; even Isaac Rosenberg greeted the outbreak of war with enthusiasm – but he, unlike Brooke, lived long enough to change his mind.)

In other respects the book is designed to promote a sense of newness. By including some anonymous poems, for instance, and some poetry written by women on the home front and elsewhere. (Readers who want to sample more of both should look at Martin Stephen's *Never Such Innocence* (Everyman, 1993), and Catherine Reilly's *Scars Upon My Heart* (Virago, 1981).) These less-familiar voices open up new perspectives. Anon's poems and songs, for instance, do more than report on the experience of 'other ranks' (virtually all the well-known war poets were officers). They capture a vitally different language, too: their ribaldry and four-letter-wording makes us realise how even Owen and Sassoon (in their more demotic pieces) and David Jones (throughout) suppressed certain sorts of authentic trench-speech in their poems, in order not to frighten off their audience.

In the same sort of way, the poetry of Margaret Postgate Cole and Eleanor Farjeon jolts our settled thoughts. It shows that trench poetry was the climax of a grim trajectory, not an entirely sealed world. Everyone knows that Owen and Sassoon looked beyond their experience of fighting, to tell people in England what conditions were really like, and to galvanise popular opposition to the war. But the proximity of peace and war, and the experience of waiting, of worrying and mourning, and of contrasting the landscape of peace with the moonscape of battle, are equally important parts of the subject. These are the elements that Edward Thomas and Ivor Gurney also made peculiarly their own, in poems which draw the home front very close to the front line. (Gurney's reputation has risen fast in the last few years, thanks largely to P. J. Kavanagh's fine edition of his poems; he is represented here as generously as he deserves to be.)

All these voices broaden our notion of what the poetry of the First World War is, and could be. They make it more various, less stereotyped, and in the process they convey its pathos to our different age. So does a third 'new' aspect to this selection. Although we are used to the idea that some of the best prose accounts of the war appeared long after it had ended, editors have been slower to point out how many poems about it continued to appear after 1918. Some by combatants (such as Blunden and Gurney) and others by people born too late to fight, who inherited strong impressions of the war from their parents and grandparents. By including some of these poems (by Ted Hughes, D. J. Enright, Glyn Maxwell and others) I have tried to show what can be gained by making a looser definition.

The purpose is not to undermine the great poets of the front line, but to re-emphasise a particular and compelling feature of their power. When Philip Larkin reviewed Owen's *Collected*

Poems in 1963 he made a judgement that helps to explain its source. 'A "war poet"', Larkin said, 'is not one who chooses to commemorate or celebrate a war, but one who reacts against having a war thrust upon him: he is chained, that is, to an historical event, and an abnormal one at that. However well he does it, however much we agree that the war happened and ought to be written about, there is still a tendency for us to withhold our highest praise on the grounds that a poet's choice of subject should seem an action, not a reaction. [G. M. Hopkins's] "The Wreck of the Deutschland", we feel, would have been markedly inferior if Hopkins had been a survivor from the passenger list.'

Larkin is right in general, insisting on the need for poets to be much more than merely anecdotal – on their need to transform, even as they describe. But he is wrong about Owen. Owen might in a sense be chained to history, but the more he regrets the fact, the more strongly he insists on remaining himself. He invokes the Keatsian tradition of lush pastoral writing, which first appeared in the early nineteenth-century as a form of celebration and benediction, and uses it to create nightmare visions of wire and craters. The result is a hideous and all-embracing irony which confirms his poems in the most fundamental way: it dramatises their sense of violation.

Owen's erotic tenderness for his fellow-soldiers works in the same way. It is at once guarded (for obvious reasons) and explicit ('I saw his round mouth's crimson . . .'), and in both respects proves the 'argument' of his poems 'on our pulses'. This mixed tone, in fact, is a kind of key to the whole operation of his poems, and a way of characterising their brilliance. His best work is at once intensely involved, and stepped-back; full of the anguish of great love poetry, and impressed by the clash and valour of conflict; immersed and independent. And it is this paradox which gives such resonance to what Ted Hughes called his 'urgently defined, practical purpose... He is not saying "Ah, God, how horrible for us!" but "Look what you've done, look!", as he presses the reader's eyes into it.'

Different forms of the same wish to act on experience appear in all the best writers here: it is what makes them the best. We see it in Sassoon's more lyrical and ruminative pieces, many of which adapt or share Owen's methods. We find it in Thomas's and Gurney's wish to write poems that are at once sharply actual, and transcendent. (In one of the prose books he wrote before the war, Thomas described himself as 'something not to be separated from the dark earth and light sky, a strong citizen of infinity and eternity'.) We have it again in Rosenberg's pictorial or sculptural devices, which give his (few, but very good) finished poems their extraordinary monumental strength, as well as their unforgettable candour.

When we speak of 'public poetry', we tend to think of poems which lead a circumscribed life. Of poems which have, as a high priority, the need to fulfil a particular social function, and which therefore make a deal with consensual language, in order to realise their aims. But the best poets of the First World War invented (or re-invented) a form of public writing in which author and subject are both immensely vulnerable, and in which language is loaded with a sense of tradition, yet stripped bare, raw, aghast at the job it has to do. Opposing the fact and management of the war, they fulfilled the public function they felt compelled to perform. At the same time, they took the whole of their terrible experience into themselves, and became exemplary.

First World War Poems

Channel Firing

That night your great guns, unawares,
Shook all our coffins as we lay,
And broke the chancel window-squares,
We thought it was the Judgment-day

And sat upright. While drearisome
Arose the howl of wakened hounds:
The mouse let fall the altar-crumb,
The worms drew back into the mounds,

The glebe cow drooled. Till God called, 'No;
It's gunnery practice out at sea
Just as before you went below;
The world is as it used to be:

'All nations striving strong to make
Red war yet redder. Mad as hatters
They do no more for Christés sake
Than you who are helpless in such matters.

'That this is not the judgment-hour
For some of them's a blessed thing,
For if it were they'd have to scour
Hell's floor for so much threatening . . .

'Ha, ha. It will be warmer when
I blow the trumpet (if indeed

I ever do; for you are men,
And rest eternal sorely need).'

So down we lay again. 'I wonder,
Will the world ever saner be,'
Said one, 'than when He sent us under
In our indifferent century!'

And many a skeleton shook his head.
'Instead of preaching forty year,'
My neighbour Parson Thirdly said,
'I wish I had stuck to pipes and beer.'

Again the guns disturbed the hour,
Roaring their readiness to avenge,
As far inland as Stourton Tower,
And Camelot, and starlit Stonehenge.

Men Who March Away

(Song of the Soldiers)

What of the faith and fire within us
    Men who march away
    Ere the barn-cocks say
    Night is growing gray,
Leaving all that here can win us;
What of the faith and fire within us
    Men who march away?

Is it a purblind prank, O think you,
    Friend with the musing eye,
    Who watch us stepping by
    With doubt and dolorous sigh?
Can much pondering so hoodwink you!
Is it a purblind prank, O think you,
    Friend with the musing eye?

Nay. We well see what we are doing,
    Though some may not see –
    Dalliers as they be –
    England's need are we;
Her distress would leave us rueing:
Nay. We well see what we are doing,
    Though some may not see!

In our heart of hearts believing
    Victory crowns the just,
    And that braggarts must

Surely bite the dust,
Press we to the field ungrieving,
In our heart of hearts believing
        Victory crowns the just.

Hence the faith and fire within us
        Men who march away
        Ere the barn-cocks say
        Night is growing gray,
Leaving all that here can win us;
Hence the faith and fire within us
        Men who march away.

THOMAS HARDY

In Time of 'The Breaking of Nations'

I

Only a man harrowing clods
    In a slow silent walk
With an old horse that stumbles and nods
    Half asleep as they stalk.

II

Only thin smoke without flame
    From the heaps of couch-grass;
Yet this will go onward the same
    Though Dynasties pass.

III

Yonder a maid and her wight
Come whispering by:
War's annals will cloud into night
Ere their story die.

The Soldier

If I should die, think only this of me:
   That there's some corner of a foreign field
That is for ever England. There shall be
   In that rich earth a richer dust concealed;
A dust whom England bore, shaped, made aware,
   Gave, once, her flowers to love, her ways to roam,
A body of England's, breathing English air,
   Washed by the rivers, blest by suns of home.

And think, this heart, all evil shed away,
   A pulse in the eternal mind, no less
     Gives somewhere back the thoughts by England given;
Her sights and sounds; dreams happy as her day;
   And laughter, learnt of friends; and gentleness,
     In hearts at peace, under an English heaven.

Train

Will the train never start?
God, make the train start.

She cannot bear it, keeping up so long;
and he, he no more tries to laugh at her.
He is going.

She holds his two hands now.
Now, she has touch of him and sight of him.
And then he will be gone.
He will be gone.

They are so young.
She stands under the window of his carriage,
and he stands in the window.
They hold each other's hands
across the window ledge.
And look and look,
and know that they may never look again.

The great clock of the station, –
how strange it is.
Terrible that the minutes go,
terrible that the minutes never go.

They had walked the platform for so long,
up and down, and up and down –

the platform, in the rainy morning,
up and down, and up and down.

The guard came by, calling,
'Take your places, take your places.'

She stands under the window of his carriage,
and he stands in the window.

God, make the train start!
Before they cannot bear it,
make the train start!

God, make the train start!

The three children, there,
in black, with the old nurse,
standing together, and looking, and looking,
up at their father in the carriage window,
they are so forlorn and silent.

The little girl will not cry,
but her chin trembles.
She throws back her head,
with its stiff little braid,
and will not cry.

Her father leans down,
out over the ledge of the window,
and kisses her, and kisses her.

She must be like her mother,
and it must be the mother who is dead.

The nurse lifts up the smallest boy,
and his father kisses him,
leaning through the carriage window.

The big boy stands very straight,
and looks at his father,
and looks, and never takes his eyes from him.
And knows that he may never look again.

Will the train never start?
God, make the train start!

The father reaches his hand down from the window,
and grips the boy's hand,
and does not speak at all.

Will the train never start?

He lets the boy's hand go.

Will the train never start?

He takes the boy's chin in his hand,
leaning out through the window,
and lifts the face that is so young, to his.
They look and look,
and know that they may never look again.

Will the train never start?
God, make the train start!

Into Battle

The naked earth is warm with spring,
  And with green grass and bursting trees
Leans to the sun's gaze glorying,
  And quivers in the sunny breeze;
And life is colour and warmth and light,
  And a striving evermore for these;
And he is dead who will not fight;
  And who dies fighting has increase.

The fighting man shall from the sun
  Take warmth, and life from the glowing earth;
Speed with the light-foot winds to run,
  And with the trees to newer birth;
And find, when fighting shall be done,
  Great rest, and fullness after dearth.

All the bright company of Heaven
  Hold him in their high comradeship,
The Dog-Star, and the Sisters Seven,
  Orion's Belt and sworded hip.

The woodland trees that stand together,
  They stand to him each one a friend;
They gently speak in the windy weather;
  They guide to valley and ridge's end.

The kestrel hovering by day,
  And the little owls that call by night,

Bid him be swift and keen as they,
  As keen of ear, as swift of sight.

The blackbird sings to him, 'Brother, brother,
  If this be the last song you shall sing,
Sing well, for you may not sing another;
  Brother, sing.'

In dreary, doubtful, waiting hours,
  Before the brazen frenzy starts,
The horses show him nobler powers;
  O patient eyes, courageous hearts!

And when the burning moment breaks,
  And all things else are out of mind,
And only joy of battle takes
  Him by the throat, and makes him blind,

Through joy and blindness he shall know,
  Not caring much to know, that still
Nor lead nor steel shall reach him, so
  That it be not the Destined Will.

The thundering line of battle stands,
  And in the air death moans and sings;
But Day shall clasp him with strong hands,
  And Night shall fold him in soft wings.

On Being Asked for a War Poem

I think it better that in times like these
A poet's mouth be silent, for in truth
We have no gift to set a statesman right;
He has had enough of meddling who can please
A young girl in the indolence of her youth,
Or an old man upon a winter's night.

An Irish Airman Foresees His Death

I know that I shall meet my fate
Somewhere among the clouds above;
Those that I fight I do not hate,
Those that I guard I do not love;
My country is Kiltartan Cross,
My countrymen Kiltartan's poor,
No likely end could bring them loss
Or leave them happier than before.
Nor law, nor duty bade me fight,
Nor public men, nor cheering crowds,
A lonely impulse of delight
Drove to this tumult in the clouds;
I balanced all, brought all to mind,
The years to come seemed waste of breath,
A waste of breath the years behind
In balance with this life, this death.

Rouen

26 April–25 May 1915

Early morning over Rouen, hopeful, high, courageous
    morning,
And the laughter of adventure and the steepness of the stair,
And the dawn across the river, and the wind across the
    bridges,
And the empty littered station and the tired people there.

Can you recall those mornings and the hurry of awakening,
And the long-forgotten wonder if we should miss the way,
And the unfamiliar faces, and the coming of provisions,
And the freshness and the glory of the labour of the day?

Hot noontide over Rouen, and the sun upon the city,
Sun and dust unceasing, and the glare of cloudless skies,
And the voices of the Indians and the endless stream of
    soldiers,
And the clicking of the tatties, and the buzzing of the flies.

Can you recall those noontides and the reek of steam and
    coffee,
Heavy-laden noontides with the evening's peace to win,
And the little piles of Woodbines, and the sticky soda bottles,
And the crushes in the 'Parlour', and the letters coming in?

Quiet night-time over Rouen, and the station full of soldiers,
All the youth and pride of England from the ends of all the
    earth;

And the rifles piled together, and the creaking of the sword-
belts,
And the faces bent above them, and the gay, heart-breaking
mirth.

Can I forget the passage from the cool white-bedded Aid Post
Past the long sun-blistered coaches of the khaki Red Cross
train
To the truck train full of wounded, and the weariness and
laughter,
And 'Good-bye, and thank you, Sister', and the empty yards
again?

Can you recall the parcels that we made them for the railroad,
Crammed and bulging parcels held together by their string,
And the voices of the sergeants who called the Drafts together,
And the agony and splendour when they stood to save the
King?

Can you forget their passing, the cheering and the waving,
The little group of people at the doorway of the shed,
The sudden awful silence when the last train swung to
darkness,
And the lonely desolation, and the mocking stars o'erhead?

Can you recall the midnights, and the footsteps of night
watchers,
Men who came from darkness and went back to dark again,
And the shadows on the rail-lines and the all-inglorious
labour,
And the promise of the daylight firing blue the window-pane?

Can you recall the passing through the kitchen door to
    morning,
Morning very still and solemn breaking slowly on the town,
And the early coastways engines that had met the ships at
    daybreak,
And the Drafts just out from England, and the day shift
    coming down?

Can you forget returning slowly, stumbling on the cobbles,
And the white-decked Red Cross barges dropping seawards
    for the tide,
And the search for English papers, and the blessed cool of
    water,
And the peace of half-closed shutters that shut out the world
    outside?

Can I forget the evenings and the sunsets on the island,
And the tall black ships at anchor far below our balcony,
And the distant call of bugles, and the white wine in the
    glasses,
And the long line of the street lamps, stretching Eastwards to
    the sea?

. . . When the world slips slow to darkness, when the office fire
    burns lower,
My heart goes out to Rouen, Rouen all the world away;
When other men remember I remember our Adventure
And the trains that go from Rouen at the ending of the day.

All the Hills and Vales Along

All the hills and vales along
Earth is bursting into song,
And the singers are the chaps
Who are going to die perhaps.
   O sing, marching men,
   Till the valleys ring again.
   Give your gladness to earth's keeping,
   So be glad, when you are sleeping.

Cast away regret and rue,
Think what you are marching to.
Little live, great pass.
Jesus Christ and Barabbas
Were found the same day.

This died, that went his way.
   So sing with joyful breath,
   For why, you are going to death.
   Teeming earth will surely store
   All the gladness that you pour.

Earth that never doubts nor fears,
Earth that knows of death, not tears,
Earth that bore with joyful ease
Hemlock for Socrates,
Earth that blossomed and was glad
'Neath the cross that Christ had,
Shall rejoice and blossom too

When the bullet reaches you.
  Wherefore, men marching
  On the road to death, sing!
  Pour your gladness on earth's head,
  So be merry, so be dead.

From the hills and valleys earth
Shouts back the sound of mirth,
Tramp of feet and lilt of song
Ringing all the road along.
All the music of their going,
Ringing swinging glad song-throwing,
Earth will echo still, when foot
Lies numb and voice mute.
  On, marching men, on
  To the gates of death with song.
  Sow your gladness for earth's reaping,
  So you may be glad, though sleeping.
  Strew your gladness on earth's bed,
  So be merry, so be dead.

Two Sonnets

I

Saints have adored the lofty soul of you.
Poets have whitened at your high renown.
We stand among the many millions who
Do hourly wait to pass your pathway down.
You, so familiar, once were strange: we tried
To live as of your presence unaware.
But now in every road on every side
We see your straight and steadfast signpost there.

I think it like that signpost in my land,
Hoary and tall, which pointed me to go
Upward, into the hills, on the right hand,
Where the mists swim and the winds shriek and blow,
A homeless land and friendless, but a land
I did not know and that I wished to know.

II

Such, such is Death: no triumph: no defeat:
Only an empty pail, a slate rubbed clean,
A merciful putting away of what has been.

And this we know: Death is not Life effete,
Life crushed, the broken pail. We who have seen
So marvellous things know well the end not yet.

Victor and vanquished are a-one in death:
Coward and brave: friend, foe. Ghosts do not say

'Come, what was your record when you drew breath?'
But a big blot has hid each yesterday
So poor, so manifestly incomplete.
And your bright Promise, withered long and sped,
Is touched, stirs, rises, opens and grows sweet
And blossoms and is you, when you are dead.

'*When you see millions . . .*'

When you see millions of the mouthless dead
Across your dreams in pale battalions go,
Say not soft things as other men have said,
That you'll remember. For you need not so.
Give them not praise. For, deaf, how should they know
It is not curses heaped on each gashed head?
Nor tears. Their blind eyes see not your tears flow.
Nor honour. It is easy to be dead.
Say only this, 'They are dead.' Then add thereto,
'Yet many a better one has died before.'
Then, scanning all the o'ercrowded mass, should you
Perceive one face that you loved heretofore,
It is a spook. None wears the face you knew.
Great death has made all his for evermore.

In Memoriam (Easter 1915)

The flowers left thick at nightfall in the wood
This Eastertide call into mind the men,
Now far from home, who, with their sweethearts, should
Have gathered them and will do never again.

'This is no case . . .'

This is no case of petty right or wrong
That politicians or philosophers
Can judge. I hate not Germans, nor grow hot
With love of Englishmen, to please newspapers.
Beside my hate for one fat patriot
My hatred of the Kaiser is love true: –
A kind of god he is, banging a gong.
But I have not to choose between the two,
Or between justice and injustice. Dinned
With war and argument I read no more
Than in the storm smoking along the wind
Athwart the wood. Two witches' cauldrons roar.
From one the weather shall rise clear and gay;
Out of the other an England beautiful
And like her mother that died yesterday.
Little I know or care if, being dull,
I shall miss something that historians
Can rake out of the ashes when perchance
The phoenix broods serene above their ken.
But with the best and meanest Englishmen
I am one in crying, God save England, lest
We lose what never slaves and cattle blessed.
The ages made her that made us from the dust:
She is all we know and live by, and we trust
She is good and must endure, loving her so:
And as we love ourselves we hate her foe.

Rain

Rain, midnight rain, nothing but the wild rain
On this bleak hut, and solitude, and me
Remembering again that I shall die
And neither hear the rain nor give it thanks
For washing me cleaner than I have been
Since I was born into this solitude.
Blessed are the dead that the rain rains upon:
But here I pray that none whom once I loved
Is dying tonight or lying still awake
Solitary, listening to the rain,
Either in pain or thus in sympathy
Helpless among the living and the dead,
Like a cold water among broken reeds,
Myriads of broken reeds all still and stiff,
Like me who have no love which this wild rain
Has not dissolved except the love of death,
If love it be towards what is perfect and
Cannot, the tempest tells me, disappoint.

Roads

I love roads:
The goddesses that dwell
Far along invisible
Are my favourite gods.

Roads go on
While we forget, and are
Forgotten like a star
That shoots and is gone.

On this earth 'tis sure
We men have not made
Anything that doth fade
So soon, so long endure:

The hill road wet with rain
In the sun would not gleam
Like a winding stream
If we trod it not again.

They are lonely
While we sleep, lonelier
For lack of the traveller
Who is now a dream only.

From dawn's twilight
And all the clouds like sheep

On the mountains of sleep
They wind into the night.

The next turn may reveal
Heaven: upon the crest
The close pine clump, at rest
And black, may Hell conceal.

Often footsore, never
Yet of the road I weary,
Though long and steep and dreary
As it winds on for ever.

Helen of the roads,
The mountain ways of Wales
And the Mabinogion tales,
Is one of the true gods,

Abiding in the trees,
The threes and fours so wise,
The larger companies,
That by the roadside be,

And beneath the rafter
Else uninhabited
Excepting by the dead;
And it is her laughter

At morn and night I hear
When the thrush cock sings
Bright irrelevant things,
And when the chanticleer

Calls back to their own night
Troops that make loneliness
With their light footsteps' press,
As Helen's own are light.

Now all roads lead to France
And heavy is the tread
Of the living; but the dead
Returning lightly dance:

Whatever the road bring
To me or take from me,
They keep me company
With their pattering,

Crowding the solitude
Of the loops over the downs,
Hushing the roar of towns
And their brief multitude.

EDWARD THOMAS

The Cherry Trees

The cherry trees bend over and are shedding
On the old road where all that passed are dead,
Their petals, strewing the grass as for a wedding
This early May morn when there is none to wed.

'The sun used to shine . . .'

The sun used to shine while we two walked
Slowly together, paused and started
Again, and sometimes mused, sometimes talked
As either pleased, and cheerfully parted

Each night. We never disagreed
Which gate to rest on. The to be
And the late past we gave small heed.
We turned from men or poetry

To rumours of the war remote
Only till both stood disinclined
For aught but the yellow flavorous coat
Of an apple wasps had undermined;

Or a sentry of dark betonies,
The stateliest of small flowers on earth,
At the forest verge; or crocuses
Pale purple as if they had their birth

In sunless Hades fields. The war
Came back to mind with the moonrise
Which soldiers in the east afar
Beheld then. Nevertheless, our eyes

Could as well imagine the Crusades
Or Caesar's battles. Everything

To faintness like those rumours fades –
Like the brook's water glittering

Under the moonlight – like those walks
Now – like us two that took them, and
The fallen apples, all the talks
And silences – like memory's sand

When the tide covers it late or soon,
And other men through other flowers
In those fields under the same moon
Go talking and have easy hours.

'As the team's head brass . . .'

As the team's head brass flashed out on the turn
The lovers disappeared into the wood.
I sat among the boughs of the fallen elm
That strewed an angle of the fallow, and
Watched the plough narrowing a yellow square
Of charlock. Every time the horses turned
Instead of treading me down, the ploughman leaned
Upon the handles to say or ask a word,
About the weather, next about the war.
Scraping the share he faced towards the wood,
And screwed along the furrow till the brass flashed
Once more.
          The blizzard felled the elm whose crest
I sat in, by a woodpecker's round hole,
The ploughman said. 'When will they take it away?'
'When the war's over.' So the talk began –
One minute and an interval of ten,
A minute more and the same interval.
'Have you been out?' 'No.' 'And don't want to, perhaps?'
'If I could only come back again, I should.
I could spare an arm. I shouldn't want to lose
A leg. If I should lose my head, why, so,
I should want nothing more . . . Have many gone
From here?' 'Yes.' 'Many lost?' 'Yes, a good few.
Only two teams work on the farm this year.
One of my mates is dead. The second day

In France they killed him. It was back in March,
The very night of the blizzard, too. Now if
He had stayed here we should have moved the tree.'
'And I should not have sat here. Everything
Would have been different. For it would have been
Another world.' 'Ay, and a better, though
If we could see all all might seem good.' Then
The lovers came out of the wood again:
The horses started and for the last time
I watched the clods crumble and topple over
After the ploughshare and the stumbling team.

EDWARD THOMAS

Lights Out

I have come to the borders of sleep,
The unfathomable deep
Forest, where all must lose
Their way, however straight
Or winding, soon or late;
They can not choose.

Many a road and track
That since the dawn's first crack
Up to the forest brink
Deceived the travellers,
Suddenly now blurs,
And in they sink.

Here love ends –
Despair, ambition ends;
All pleasure and all trouble,
Although most sweet or bitter,
Here ends, in sleep that is sweeter
Than tasks most noble.

There is not any book
Or face of dearest look
That I would not turn from now
To go into the unknown
I must enter, and leave, alone,
I know not how.

The tall forest towers:
Its cloudy foliage lowers
Ahead, shelf above shelf:
Its silence I hear and obey
That I may lose my way
And myself.

ELEANOR FARJEON

Easter Monday
(In Memoriam E.T.)

In the last letter that I had from France
You thanked me for the silver Easter egg
Which I had hidden in the box of apples
You liked to munch beyond all other fruit.
You found the egg the Monday before Easter,
And said, 'I will praise Easter Monday now –
It was such a lovely morning.' Then you spoke
Of the coming battle and said, 'This is the eve.
Good-bye. And may I have a letter soon.'

That Easter Monday was a day for praise,
It was such a lovely morning. In our garden
We sowed our earliest seeds, and in the orchard
The apple-bud was ripe. It was the eve.
There are three letters that you will not get.

Concert Party: Busseboom

The stage was set, the house was packed,
    The famous troop began;
Our laughter thundered, act by act;
    Time light as sunbeams ran.

Dance sprang and spun and neared and fled,
    Jest chirped at gayest pitch,
Rhythm dazzled, action sped
    Most comically rich.

With generals and lame privates both
    Such charms worked wonders, till
The show was over – lagging loth
    We faced the sunset chill;

And standing on the sandy way,
    With the cracked church peering past,
We heard another matinée,
    We heard the maniac blast

Of barrage south by Saint Eloi,
    And the red lights flaming there
Called madness: Come, my bonny boy,
    And dance to the latest air.

To this new concert, white we stood;
    Cold certainty held our breath;
While men in the tunnels below Larch Wood
    Were kicking men to death.

Pillbox

Just see what's happening, Worley! – Worley rose
And round the angled doorway thrust his nose
And Serjeant Hoad went too to snuff the air.
Then war brought down his fist, and missed the pair!
Yet Hoad was scratched by a splinter, the blood came,
And out burst terrors that he'd striven to tame,
A good man, Hoad, for weeks. *I'm blown to bits,*
He groans, he screams. *Come, Bluffer, where's your wits?*
Says Worley, *Bluffer, you've a blighty, man!*
And in the pillbox urged him, here began
His freedom: *Think of Eastbourne and your dad.*
The poor man lay at length and brief and mad
Flung out his cry of doom; soon ebbed and dumb
He yielded. Worley with a tot of rum
And shouting in his face could not restore him.
The ship of Charon over channel bore him.
All marvelled even on that most deathly day
To see this life so spirited away.

Festubert, 1916

Tired with dull grief, grown old before my day,
I sit in solitude and only hear
Long silent laughters, murmurings of dismay,
The lost intensities of hope and fear;
In those old marshes yet the rifles lie,
On the thin breastwork flutter the grey rags,
The very books I read are there – and I
Dead as the men I loved, wait while life drags

Its wounded length from those sad streets of war
Into green places here, that were my own;
But now what once was mine is mine no more,
I look for such friends here and I find none.
With such strong gentleness and tireless will
Those ruined houses seared themselves in me,
Passionate I look for their dumb story still,
And the charred stub outspeaks the living tree.

I rise up at the singing of a bird
And scarcely knowing slink along the lane,
I dare not give a soul a look or word
For all have homes and none's at home in vain:
Deep red the rose burned in the grim redoubt,
The self-sown wheat around was like a flood,
In the hot path the lizard lolled time out,
The saints in broken shrines were bright as blood.

Sweet Mary's shrine between the sycamores!
There we would go, my friend of friends and I,
And snatch long moments from the grudging wars;
Whose dark made light intense to see them by . . .
Shrewd bit the morning fog, the whining shots
Spun from the wrangling wire; then in warm swoon
The sun hushed all but the cool orchard plots,
We crept in the tall grass and slept till noon.

'Transport Up' at Ypres

The thoroughfares that seem so dead to daylight passers-by
Change character when the dark comes down, and traffic
    starts to ply;
Never a noisier street than the Rue de Malou then becomes
With the cartwheels jolting the dead awake, and the cars like
    rumbling drums.

The crazy houses watch them pass, and stammer with the
    roar,
The drivers hustle on their mules, more come behind and
    more;
Briskly the black mules clatter by, to-day was Devil's Mass;
The loathly smell of picric here, and there a touch of gas.

From silhouettes to pitchy blur, beneath the bitter stars,
The interminable convoy streams of horses, vans and cars.
They clamour through the cheerless night, the streets a
    slattern maze,
The sentries at the corners shout them on their different ways.

And so they go, night after night, and chance the shrapnel fire,
The sappers' waggons stowed with frames and concertina
    wire,
The ration-limbers for the line, the lorries for the guns:
While overhead with fleering light stare down those withered
    suns.

The Veteran
May, 1916

We came upon him sitting in the sun,
  Blinded by war, and left. And past the fence
There came young soldiers from the Hand and Flower,
  Asking advice of his experience.

And he said this, and that, and told them tales,
  And all the nightmares of each empty head
Blew into air; then, hearing us beside,
  'Poor chaps, how'd they know what it's like?' he said.

And we stood there, and watched him as he sat,
  Turning his sockets where they went away,
Until it came to one of us to ask
  'And you're – how old?'
    'Nineteen, the third of May.'

Praematuri

When men are old, and their friends die,
They are not so sad,
Because their love is running slow,
And cannot spring from the wound with so sharp a pain;
And they are happy with many memories,
And only a little while to be alone.

But we are young, and our friends are dead
Suddenly, and our quick love is torn in two;
So our memories are only hopes that came to nothing.
We are left alone like old men; we should be dead
– But there are years and years in which we shall still be young.

The Legion

'Is that the Three-and-Twentieth, Strabo mine,
Marching below, and we still gulping wine?'
From the sad magic of his fragrant cup
The red-faced old centurion started up,
Cursed, battered on the table. 'No,' he said,
'Not that! The Three-and-Twentieth Legion's dead,
Dead in the first year of this damned campaign –
The Legion's dead, dead, and won't rise again.
Pity? Rome pities her brave lads that die,
But we need pity also, you and I,
Whom Gallic spear and Belgian arrow miss,
Who live to see the Legion come to this,
Unsoldierlike, slovenly, bent on loot,
Grumblers, diseased, unskilled to thrust or shoot.
O brown cheek, muscled shoulder, sturdy thigh!
Where are they now? God! watch it straggle by,
The sullen pack of ragged ugly swine.
Is that the Legion, Gracchus? Quick, the wine!'
'Strabo,' said Gracchus, 'you are strange tonight.
The Legion is the Legion, it's all right.
If these new men are slovenly, in your thinking,
Hell take it! you'll not better them by drinking.
They all try, Strabo; trust their hearts and hands.
The Legion is the Legion while Rome stands,
And these same men before the autumn's fall
Shall bang old Vercingetorix out of Gaul.'

Breakfast

We ate our breakfast lying on our backs
Because the shells were screeching overhead.
I bet a rasher to a loaf of bread
That Hull United would beat Halifax
When Jimmy Stainthorpe played full-back instead
Of Billy Bradford. Ginger raised his head
And cursed, and took the bet, and dropt back dead.
We ate our breakfast lying on our backs
Because the shells were screeching overhead.

Mark Anderson

On the low table by the bed
Where it was set aside last night,
Beyond the bandaged lifeless head,
It glitters in the morning light;

And as the hours of watching pass,
I cannot sleep, I cannot think,
But only gaze upon the glass
Of water that he could not drink.

A Lament

We who are left, how shall we look again
Happily on the sun or feel the rain,
Without remembering how they who went
Ungrudgingly and spent
Their all for us loved, too, the sun and rain?

A bird among the rain-wet lilac sings –
But we, how shall we turn to little things
And listen to the birds and winds and streams
Made holy by their dreams,
Nor feel the heart-break in the heart of things?

from *Picnic*

July 1917

We lay and ate sweet hurt-berries
    In the bracken of Hurt Wood.
Like a quire of singers singing low
    The dark pines stood.

Behind us climbed the Surrey hills,
    Wild, wild in greenery;
At our feet the downs of Sussex broke
    To an unseen sea.

And life was bound in a still ring,
    Drowsy, and quiet, and sweet . . .
When heavily up the south-east wind
    The great guns beat.

We did not wince, we did not weep,
    We did not curse or pray;
We drowsily heard, and someone said,
    'They sound clear today.'

We did not shake with pity and pain,
    Or sicken and blanch white.
We said, 'If the wind's from over there
    There'll be rain tonight.'

from *Kneeshaw Goes to War*

4

There are a few left who will find it hard to forget
Polygonveld.
The earth was scarr'd and broken
By torrents of plunging shells;
Then wash'd and sodden with autumnal rains.
And Polygonbeke
(Perhaps a rippling stream
In the days of Kneeshaw's gloom)
Spread itself like a fatal quicksand, –
A sucking, clutching death.
They had to be across the beke
And in their line before dawn.
A man who was marching by Kneeshaw's side
Hesitated in the middle of the mud,
And slowly sank, weighted down by equipment and arms.
He cried for help;
Rifles were stretched to him;
He clutched and they tugged,
But slowly he sank.
His terror grew –
Grew visibly when the viscous ooze
Reached his neck.

And there he seemed to stick,
Sinking no more.
They could not dig him out –
The oozing mud would flow back again.

The dawn was very near.

An officer shot him through the head:
Not a neat job – the revolver
Was too close.

Winter Warfare

Colonel Cold strode up the Line
    (tabs of rime and spurs of ice);
stiffened all who met his glare:
    horses, men, and lice.

Visited a forward post,
    left them burning, ear to foot;
fingers stuck to biting steel,
    toes to frozen boot.

Stalked on into No Man's Land,
    turned the wire to fleecy wool,
iron stakes to sugar sticks
    snapping at a pull.

Those who watched with hoary eyes
    saw two figures gleaming there;
Hauptman Kalte, Colonel Cold,
    gaunt in the grey air.

Stiffly, tinkling spurs they moved,
    glassy eyed, with glinting heel
stabbing those who lingered there
    torn by screaming steel.

from *In Parenthesis, Part 4*

The storeman found the complement correct. In half an hour they were back in the fire-trench traverses.

Corporal Quilter gave them no formal dismissal, nor did he enquire further what duties his party might next perform. Each one of them disposed himself in some part of their few yards of trench, and for an hour or more were left quite undisturbed, to each his own business. To talk together of the morning's affairs; to fall easily to sleep; to search for some personally possessed thing, wedged tightly between articles drawn from the Quartermaster; to re-read yet again the last arrived letter; to see if the insistent water were penetrated within the stout valise canvas, sufficiently to make useless the very thing you could do with; to look at illustrations in last week's limp and soiled *Graphic*, of Christmas preparations with the Fleet, and full-page portraits of the High Command; to be assured that the spirit of the troops is excellent, that the nation proceeds confidently in its knowledge of victory, that Miss Ashwell would perform before all ranks, that land-girls stamp like girls in Luna.

The two Joneses were in argument.

Private Ball groped in his pack to find his book. The India paper was abominably adhered, especially for split finger-tips – and one anthology is as bad as a library and there is no new thing under the sun.

> *Takis, on the motheris breast sowkand,*
> *The babe full of benignitie:–*

> .　　　.　　　.

> *He takis the campion in the stour,*
>
> .   .   .
>
> *He has tane Rowll of Aberdene,*
> *And gentill Rowll of Corstorphine;*
> *Two better fallowis did no man see: –*

He closed the book – he would eat some chocolate.

Aneirin Lewis sat motionless in the far corner of the bay. The man from Rotherhithe looked to the well-being of his mouth-organ. Private Watcyn was trying to read the scores on the reverse side of Private Thomas's *Western Mail* – as do men in railway carriages. Bobby Saunders slept.

The midday quietness was quite unbroken. They changed sentries at five minutes to the hour, and even this was done without a word for the 'relief' or the 'relieved', regardless of proper usage. A faulty detonated 4.2 deranged the picketed wire outside the trench as the new sentry took over, making him hug closer the parapet, in expectation; but the capricious gunners let be at that, for their ways are inscrutable.

The day wore on without any happening. The sun unseen reached his low meridian. They ate what bread remained from breakfast and opened tins of beef, and more successfully made some tea. The feebleness of before-noon abated, gave place to an after-lunch content. With the passing hours the wind backed from south to south-east to east. Men sneezed, it grew noticeably colder. The sentry at the Gas Post put up the Alert notice. They were almost eager when required to fill sandbags to repair a freshly destroyed defence. They warmed to their work, and found some interest in this remaking. They strengthened their hands like the builders at the watergate, and everyone wore his harness and so builded other than the watcher at the fire-step, who saw mirrored a new influence break the topmost headers of his parapets; and creep down

[55]

that dun hostile wall and bathe the rusted tangle of his outer belt – now sweep all the waste with horizontal beam.

Hidden since the dawn he shines at his departing: fretted like captive-fire at boundary-mound. Each interstice burned between lath and common rafter – each cranny bright, where four walls yet held precariously, purlin and principal, far away over, beyond the parados, in the west.

Tomorrow, before daybreak, a ranging heavy will find the foundations and leave the kitchen flooring pounded like red-pepper, with Cecile's school satchel still hanging at its peg; and the Papal Blessing punctured in its gimcrack frame, poking from the midden. Ober-Leutnant Müller will be blamed for failing to locate a British battery.

The watcher at the fire-step began to hope that his friends would so make an end of their work as to spread their tea-napery of news-sheets, to make the dixie boil to synchronise with his relief.

The last direct radiance gave out, his wire and rising glacis went cold and unillumined, yet clearly defined, in an evenly distributed after-visibility. The cratered earth, of all growing things bereaved, bore that uncreaturely impressiveness of telescope-observed bodies – where even pterodactyl would feel the place unfriendly.

His mates came from the building-up, and work of restoration; the watched dixie almost boiled. Watcyn had already opened the *Dairymaid* canned butter, it was just light enough to know the green and gilt of the enamelled tin. It was an extremely good brand. The light from their gusty culinary flame began to tell warmly on the nearer surfaces. The walls with the skeleton roof stood quite black now against an even clearness, and showed for the last time what remained of that unity intended of their builders. The sky overhead looked crisp as eggshell, wide-domed of porcelain, that suddenly would fracture to innumerable stars. The thin mud on the fire-steps slats glistened, sharpened into rime. The up-to-ankle water became intolerably cold. Two men hasten from the communication trench. They deposit grenade-boxes in a recess used for that purpose and quickly go away. A young man in a British warm, his fleecy muffler cosy to his ears, enquired if anyone had seen the Liaison Officer from Corps, as one who asks of the Tube-lift man at Westminster the whereabouts of the Third Sea Lord. Vacant faces turned to him. He was advised to try Mr Jenkins in the sap. He turned again, the way he came. Sergeant Snell hurried along the trench carrying a Véry-light pistol; he detailed four men for company rations as he passed. The man with the loose tea and sugar shook some part of it from the sack into the boiling water; and as he poured he heard unmistakable words, near-ing, traverse by traverse from the right.

Mr Jenkins was back from the sap:

Drink that stuff quickly and stand-to.

He is away again with no other word.

No-man's-land whitened rigid: all its contours silver filigreed, as damascened. With the coming dark, ground-mist creeps back to regain the hollow places; across the rare atmosphere you could hear foreign men cough, and stamp with foreign feet. Things seen precisely just now lost exactness. Biez wood became only a darker shape uncertainly expressed. Your eyes begin to strain after escaping definitions. Whether that picket-iron moved toward or some other fell away, or after all is it an animate thing just there by the sap-head or only the slight frosted-sway of suspended wire.

A long way off a machine-gunner seemed as one tuning an instrument, who strikes the same note quickly, several times, and now a lower one, singly; while scene-shifters thud and scrape behind expectant curtaining; and impatient shuffling of the feet – in the stalls they take out watches with a nervous hand, they can hardly bear it.

Now the fixed-riflemen take notice: it is almost time for ration-parties to perambulate the road.

The first star tremored: her fragile ray as borne on quivering exsultet-reed. From Gretchen Trench lights begin to rise, the first to splutter out, ill discharged.

Have you seen grinning boys fumble with points of flame who blame the taper's damp. At last, one adequately fused, soars competently up in hurrying challenge, to stand against that admirable bright, as crystal cut, lit singly to herald the immediateness of night.

In a quarter of an hour it was quite dark.

You are told to stand-down.

Night-sentries are posted in twos.

Men detailed are to report at once.

Messages drift from bay to bay.

Pass it along – Mr Prys-Picton's patrol will go out at 8.30 from Pope's Nose and will return by the Sally-Port. Sentries will not fire in this area.

The countersign is 'Harlequin'.

The Lewis-team by the road are experimenting through their newly enlarged loop-hole.

Fans of orange light broke in dancing sequence beyond his lines.

Bursts in groups of four jarred the frosted air with ringing sound.

Brittle discord waft back from the neighbourhood of the Richebourg truckway.

Guns of swift response opened on his back areas. In turn his howitzers coal-boxed the Supports.

So gathered with uneven pulse the night-antiphonal: mortared-canisters careened oblique descent with meteor trail; and men were dumb and held their breath for this, as for no thing other.

In the next sector the continued vibrating developed greater weight.

High signal-flares shot up to agitate the starred serenity: red and green and white.

The N.C.O. at the Gas Post looked to his apparatus, and placed in a convenient sequence his ready rocket-gear.

But it peters out; and with the lull they speak to each other.

The sentries stand more erect.

They whistle, softly.

Solitary star-shells toss as the dark deepens.

Mr Prys-Picton's patrol came in, well before midnight.

Epitaph on an Army of Mercenaries

These, in the day when heaven was falling,
　The hour when earth's foundations fled,
Followed their mercenary calling
　And took their wages and are dead.

Their shoulders held the sky suspended;
　They stood, and earth's foundations stay;
What God abandoned, these defended,
　And saved the sum of things for pay.

ANONYMOUS

For You but not for Me
(The Bells of Hell)

The Bells of Hell go ting-a-ling-a-ling
For you but not for me;
And the little devils how they sing-a-ling-a-ling
For you but not for me.
O Death, where is thy sting-a-ling-a-ling,
O Grave, thy victory?
The Bells of Hell go ting-a-ling-a ling
For you but not for me.

ANONYMOUS

Song

Do your balls hang low?
Do they dangle to and fro?
Can you tie them in a knot?
Can you tie them in a bow?

Do they rattle when you walk?
Do they jingle when you talk?

Do they itch when it's hot?
Do you rest them in a pot?

Can you sling them on your shoulder
Like a lousy fucking soldier?
DO YOUR BALLS HANG LOW?

I Don't Want to be a Soldier
(Air: 'On Sunday I Walk Out With a Soldier')

I don't want to be a soldier,
I don't want to go to war.
I'd rather stay at home,
Around the streets to roam,
And live on the earnings of a well-paid whore.
I don't want a bayonet up my arse-hole,
I don't want my ballocks shot away.
I'd rather stay in England,
In merry merry England,
And fuck my bloody life away.

Tiddleywinks, Old Man
(Air: Hornpipe)

Tiddleywinks, old man,
Find a woman if you can.
If you can't find a woman,
Do without, old man.
When the Rock of Gibraltar
Takes a flying leap at Malta,
You'll never get your ballocks in a corn-beef can.

The Old Battalion

If you want to find the sergeant,
I know where he is, I know where he is;
If you want to find the sergeant,
I know where he is:
He's lying on the canteen floor.
I've seen him, I've seen him,
Lying on the canteen floor.
I've seen him,
Lying on the canteen floor.

If you want to find the quarter-bloke,
I know where he is, I know where he is;
If you want to find the quarter-bloke,
I know where he is:
He's miles and miles behind the line.
I've seen him, I've seen him,
Miles and miles behind the line.
I've seen him,
Miles and miles behind the line.

If you want to find the sergeant-major,
I know where he is, I know where he is;
If you want to find the sergeant-major,
I know where he is:
He's boozing up the privates' rum.
I've seen him, I've seen him,
Boozing up the privates' rum.

I've seen him,
Boozing up the privates' rum.

If you want to find the CO,
I know where he is, I know where he is;
If you want to find the CO,
I know where he is:
He's down in the deep dugouts.
I've seen him, I've seen him,
Down in the deep dugouts.
I've seen him,
Down in the deep dugouts.

If you want to find the old battalion,
I know where they are, I know where they are;
If you want to find the old battalion,
I know where they are:
They're hanging on the old barbed wire.
I've seen them, I've seen them,
Hanging on the old barbed wire.
I've seen them,
Hanging on the old barbed wire.

ANONYMOUS

To Little Sister
From No. 16

Have you seen our Little Sister?
Officers can ne'er resist her.
She will flay and burn and blister
Someone every day.

Does she tend poor wounded wretches?
No! Their wounds she probes and stretches
Till the brandy flask she fetches
When they faint away.

Not for them the gentle touches
Of a Matron or a Duchess –
Little Sister simply BUTCHERS
Everyone she gets.
Rubber gloves her hands adorning
Give to us a daily warning
That the bone she cleans each morning
Never, never sets.

Though our misery's unending,
Though with pain our wounds she's tending,
Yet with courage still unbending
We can bear the strain.
But if once we woke and missed her
We should cry with tears that blister,
'Have you seen our Little Sister?
Send her back again!'

Song

Only the wanderer
　　Knows England's graces,
Or can anew see clear
　　Familiar faces.

And who loves joy as he
　　That dwells in shadows?
Do not forget me quite,
　　O Severn meadows.

To His Love

He's gone, and all our plans
   Are useless indeed.
We'll walk no more on Cotswold
   Where the sheep feed
   Quietly and take no heed.

His body that was so quick
   Is not as you
Knew it, on Severn river
   Under the blue
   Driving our small boat through.

You would not know him now . . .
   But still he died
Nobly, so cover him over
   With violets of pride
   Purple from Severn side.

Cover him, cover him soon!
   And with thick-set
Masses of memoried flowers –
   Hide that red wet
   Thing I must somehow forget.

First Time In

After the dread tales and red yarns of the Line
Anything might have come to us; but the divine
Afterglow brought us up to a Welsh colony
Hiding in sandbag ditches, whispering consolatory
Soft foreign things. Then we were taken in
To low huts candle-lit, shaded close by slitten
Oilsheets, and there the boys gave us kind welcome,
So that we looked out as from the edge of home,
Sang us Welsh things, and changed all former notions
To human hopeful things. And the next day's guns
Nor any line-pangs ever quite could blot out
That strangely beautiful entry to war's rout;
Candles they gave us, precious and shared over-rations –
Ulysses found little more in his wanderings without doubt.
'David of the White Rock', the 'Slumber Song' so soft, and that
Beautiful tune to which roguish words by Welsh pit boys
Are sung– but never more beautiful than there under the guns'
    noise.

After War

One got peace of heart at last, the dark march over,
And the straps slipped, the warmth felt under roof's low cover,
Lying slack the body, let sink in straw giving;
And some sweetness, a great sweetness felt in mere living.
And to come to this haven after sorefooted weeks,
The dark barn roof, and the glows and the wedges and streaks;
Letters from home, dry warmth and still sure rest taken
Sweet to the chilled frame, nerves soothed were so sore shaken.

The Silent One

Who died on the wires, and hung there, one of two –
Who for his hours of life had chattered through
Infinite lovely chatter of Bucks accent:
Yet faced unbroken wires; stepped over, and went
A noble fool, faithful to his stripes – and ended.
But I weak, hungry, and willing only for the chance
Of line – to fight in the line, lay down under unbroken
Wires, and saw the flashes and kept unshaken,
Till the politest voice – a finicking accent, said:
'Do you think you might crawl through there: there's a hole.'
Darkness, shot at: I smiled, as politely replied –
'I'm afraid not, Sir.' There was no hole no way to be seen
Nothing but chance of death, after tearing of clothes.
Kept flat, and watched the darkness, hearing bullets whizzing –
And thought of music – and swore deep heart's deep oaths
(Polite to God) and retreated and came on again,
Again retreated – and a second time faced the screen.

Strange Hells

There are strange Hells within the minds War made
Not so often, not so humiliatingly afraid
As one would have expected – the racket and fear guns made.

One Hell the Gloucester soldiers they quite put out;
Their first bombardment, when in combined black shout
Of fury, guns aligned, they ducked low their heads
And sang with diaphragms fixed beyond all dreads,
That tin and stretched-wire tinkle, that blither of tune;
'Après la guerre fini' till Hell all had come down,
Twelve-inch, six-inch, and eighteen pounders hammering
    Hell's thunders.

Where are they now on State-doles, or showing shop patterns
Or walking town to town sore in borrowed tatters
Or begged. Some civic routine one never learns.
The heart burns – but has to keep out of face how heart burns.

The Interview

Death I have often faced
In the damp trench – or poisoned waste:
Shell or shot, gas or flying steel, bayonet –
But only once by one bullet my arm was wet
With blood. Death faced me there, Death it was that I faced.
But now by no means may it come to me.
Mercy of Death noways vouchsafed to pain.
Were but those times of battle to come again!
Or even boat-sailing, danger on a mimic inland sea!
Death moaning, Death flying, shrieking in air.
Desiring its mark sufficient everywhere – everywhere.
Interview enough. But now I can not get near
Such challenge or dear enmity; pain more than fear
Oppresses me – would that might come again!
Death in the narrow trench . . . or wide in the fields.
Death in the Reserve, where the earth wild beautiful flowers
    yields.
Death met – outfaced – but here – not to be got.
Prayed for, truly desired, obtainèd not –
A lot past dreadfulness, an unhuman lot.
For never Man was meant to be denied chance
Of ending pain past strength – O for France! for France!
Death walked freely; one might be sought of him
Or seek, in twilight or first light of morning dim.
Death dreadful that scared the cheeks of blood;
Took friends, spoilt any happy true-human mood;
Shrieked in the near air – threatened from up on high.
Dreadful, dreadful. But not to be come by

Now, confined – no Interview is ever here.
And worse than Death is known in the spirit of fear.
Death is a thing desired, never to be had at all –
Spirit for Death cries, nothing hears; nothing granted here. O
If Mercy would but hear the cry of the spirit grow
From waking till Death seems far beyond a right,
And dark is the spirit that has all right to be bright.
Death is not here, save mercy grant it. When
Was cruelty such known last among like-and-like men?
An Interview? It is cried for – and not known –
Not found. Death absent what thing is truly man's own?
Beaten down continually, continually beaten clean down.

The Mangel-Bury

It was after war; Edward Thomas had fallen at Arras –
I was walking by Gloucester musing on such things
As fill his verse with goodness; it was February; the long house
Straw-thatched of the mangels stretched two wide wings;
And looked as part of the earth heaped up by dead soldiers
In the most fitting place – along the hedge's yet-bare lines.
West spring breathed there early, that none foreign divines.
Across the flat country the rattling of the cart sounded;
Heavy of wood, jingling of iron; as he neared me I waited
For the chance perhaps of heaving at those great rounded
Ruddy or orange things – and right to be rolled and hefted
By a body like mine, soldier still, and clean from water.
Silent he assented; till the cart was drifted
High with those creatures, so right in size and matter.
We threw them with our bodies swinging, blood in my ears
    singing;
His was the thick-set sort of farmer, but well-built –
Perhaps, long before, his blood's name ruled all,
Watched all things for his own. If my luck had so willed
Many questions of lordship I had heard him tell – old
Names, rumours. But my pain to more moving called
And him to some barn business far in the fifteen acre field.

The Bohemians

Certain people would not clean their buttons,
Nor polish buckles after latest fashions,
Preferred their hair long, putties comfortable,
Barely escaping hanging, indeed hardly able,
In Bridge and smoking without army cautions
Spending hours that sped like evil for quickness,
(While others burnished brasses, earned promotions)
These were those ones who jested in the trench,
While others argued of army ways, and wrenched
What little soul they had still further from shape,
And died off one by one, or became officers
Without the first of dream, the ghost of notions
Of ever becoming soldiers, or smart and neat,
Surprised as ever to find the army capable
Of sounding 'Lights out' to break a game of Bridge,
As to fear candles would set a barn alight.
In Artois or Picardy they lie – free of useless fashions.

Varennes

At Varennes also Gloucester men had their stay.
(Infantry again, of my soft job getting tired.)
Saw wonderful things of full day and of half-day:
Black pattern of twigs against the sunset dim fired;
Stars like quick inspirations of God in the seven o'clock sky.
Where the infantry drilled frozen – all all foolishly
As on the Plain – but to the canteen went I,
Got there by high favour, having run, finished third,
In a mile race from Varennes to the next village end.
Canteen assistant, with a special care for B Company –
And biscuits hidden for favour in a manner forbidden.
Lying about chocolate to C Company hammering the gate.
Pitying them for their parades all the morning through
(Blue to the fingers, to all but the conscience blue)
Uselessly doing fatheaded things eternally.
But keeping (as was natural) Six Platoon ever in mind.
And one evening, drowsed by the wood fire I got lost in the
Blaze of warm embers, green wood smoking annoyingly;
Watched deep till my soul in the magic was rapt asleep:
Grew to power of music, and all poetries, so, uncared,
Became a maker among soldiers – dear comrades;
Which is the hardest of all wide earth's many trades;
And so proved my birthright, in a minute of warm aired
Staring into the woodfire's poetic heart, lost a tide deep.
(Until the anger of fire caught all, all in rose or gold was lost.)

War Books

What did they expect of our toil and extreme
Hunger – the perfect drawing of a heart's dream?
Did they look for a book of wrought art's perfection,
Who promised no reading, nor praise, nor publication?
Out of the heart's sickness the spirit wrote
For delight, or to escape hunger, or of war's worst anger,
When the guns died to silence and men would gather sense
Somehow together, and find this was life indeed,
And praise another's nobleness, or to Cotswold get hence.
There we wrote – Corbie Ridge – or in Gonnehem at rest –
Or Fauquissart – our world's death songs, ever the best.
One made sorrows' praise passing the church where silence
Opened for the long quivering strokes of the bell –
Another wrote all soldiers' praise, and of France and night's
    stars,
Served his guns, got immortality, and died well.
But Ypres played another trick with its danger on me,
Kept still the needing and loving-of-action body,
Gave no candles, and nearly killed me twice as well,
And no souvenirs, though I risked my life in the stuck tanks.
Yet there was praise of Ypres, love came sweet in hospital,
And old Flanders went under to long ages of plays' thought in
    my pages.

Break of Day in the Trenches

The darkness crumbles away –
It is the same old druid Time as ever.
Only a live thing leaps my hand –
A queer sardonic rat –
As I pull the parapet's poppy
To stick behind my ear.
Droll rat, they would shoot you if they knew
Your cosmopolitan sympathies.
Now you have touched this English hand
You will do the same to a German –
Soon, no doubt, if it be your pleasure
To cross the sleeping green between.
It seems you inwardly grin as you pass
Strong eyes, fine limbs, haughty athletes
Less chanced than you for life,
Bonds to the whims of murder,
Sprawled in the bowels of the earth,
The torn fields of France.
What do you see in our eyes
At the shrieking iron and flame
Hurled through still heavens?
What quaver – what heart aghast?
Poppies whose roots are in man's veins
Drop, and are ever dropping;
But mine in my ear is safe,
Just a little white with the dust.

Louse Hunting

Nudes – stark and glistening,
Yelling in lurid glee. Grinning faces
And raging limbs
Whirl over the floor one fire.
For a shirt verminously busy
Yon soldier tore from his throat, with oaths
Godhead might shrink at, but not the lice.
And soon the shirt was aflare
Over the candle he'd lit while we lay.

Then we all sprang up and stript
To hunt the verminous brood.
Soon like a demons' pantomime
The place was raging.
See the silhouettes agape,
See the gibbering shadows
Mixed with the battled arms on the wall.
See gargantuan hooked fingers
Pluck in supreme flesh
To smutch supreme littleness.
See the merry limbs in hot Highland fling
Because some wizard vermin
Charmed from the quiet this revel
When our ears were half lulled
By the dark music
Blown from Sleep's trumpet.

Returning, We Hear the Larks

Sombre the night is.
And though we have our lives, we know
What sinister threat lurks there.

Dragging these anguished limbs, we only know
This poison-blasted track opens on our camp –
On a little safe sleep.

But hark! joy – joy – strange joy.
Lo! heights of night ringing with unseen larks.
Music showering on our upturned list'ning faces.

Death could drop from the dark
As easily as song –
But song only dropped,
Like a blind man's dreams on the sand
By dangerous tides,
Like a girl's dark hair for she dreams no ruin lies there,
Or her kisses where a serpent hides.

ISAAC ROSENBERG

Dead Man's Dump

The plunging limbers over the shattered track
Racketed with their rusty freight,
Stuck out like many crowns of thorns,
And the rusty stakes like sceptres old
To stay the flood of brutish men
Upon our brothers dear.

The wheels lurched over sprawled dead
But pained them not, though their bones crunched,
Their shut mouths made no moan.
They lie there huddled, friend and foeman,
Man born of man, and born of woman,
And shells go crying over them
From night till night and now.

Earth has waited for them,
All the time of their growth
Fretting for their decay:
Now she has them at last!
In the strength of their strength
Suspended – stopped and held.

What fierce imaginings their dark souls lit?
Earth! have they gone into you!
Somewhere they must have gone,
And flung on your hard back
Is their soul's sack

Emptied of God-ancestralled essences.
Who hurled them out? Who hurled?

None saw their spirits' shadow shake the grass,
Or stood aside for the half used life to pass
Out of those doomed nostrils and the doomed mouth,
When the swift iron burning bee
Drained the wild honey of their youth.

What of us who, flung on the shrieking pyre,
Walk, our usual thoughts untouched,
Our lucky limbs as on ichor fed,
Immortal seeming ever?
Perhaps when the flames beat loud on us,
A fear may choke in our veins
And the startled blood may stop.

The air is loud with death,
The dark air spurts with fire,
The explosions ceaseless are.
Timelessly now, some minutes past,
These dead strode time with vigorous life,
Till the shrapnel called 'An end!'
But not to all. In bleeding pangs
Some borne on stretchers dreamed of home,
Dear things, war-blotted from their hearts.

Maniac Earth! howling and flying, your bowel
Seared by the jagged fire, the iron love,
The impetuous storm of savage love.
Dark Earth! dark Heavens! swinging in chemic smoke,
What dead are born when you kiss each soundless soul

With lightning and thunder from your mined heart,
Which man's self dug, and his blind fingers loosed?

A man's brains splattered on
A stretcher-bearer's face;
His shook shoulders slipped their load,
But when they bent to look again
The drowning soul was sunk too deep
For human tenderness.

They left this dead with the older dead,
Stretched at the cross roads.

Burnt black by strange decay
Their sinister faces lie,
The lid over each eye,
The grass and coloured clay
More motion have than they,
Joined to the great sunk silences.

Here is one not long dead;
His dark hearing caught our far wheels,
And the choked soul stretched weak hands
To reach the living word the far wheels said,
The blood-dazed intelligence beating for light,
Crying through the suspense of the far torturing wheels
Swift for the end to break
Or the wheels to break,
Cried as the tide of the world broke over his sight.

Will they come? Will they ever come?
Even as the mixed hoofs of the mules,
The quivering-bellied mules,

And the rushing wheels all mixed
With his tortured upturned sight.
So we crashed round the bend,
We heard his weak scream,
We heard his very last sound,
And our wheels grazed his dead face.

A Working Party

Three hours ago he blundered up the trench,
Sliding and poising, groping with his boots;
Sometimes he tripped and lurched against the walls
With hands that pawed the sodden bags of chalk.
He couldn't see the man who walked in front;
Only he heard the drum and rattle of feet
Stepping along barred trench-boards, often splashing
Wretchedly where the sludge was ankle-deep.

Voices would grunt 'Keep to your right – make way!'
When squeezing past some men from the front line:
White faces peered, puffing a point of red;
Candles and braziers glinted through the chinks
And curtain-flaps of dug-outs; then the gloom
Swallowed his sense of sight; he stopped and swore
Because a sagging wire had caught his neck.

A flare went up; the shining whiteness spread
And flickered upward, showing nimble rats
And mounds of glimmering sandbags, bleached with rain;
Then the slow silver moment died in dark.
The wind came posting by with chilly gusts
And buffeting at corners, piping thin
And dreary through the crannies; rifle-shots
Would split and crack and sing along the night,
And shells came calmly through the drizzling air
To burst with hollow bang below the hill.

Three hours ago he stumbled up the trench;
Now he will never walk that road again:
He must be carried back, a jolting lump
Beyond all need of tenderness and care.

He was a young man with a meagre wife
And two small children in a Midland town;
He showed their photographs to all his mates,
And they considered him a decent chap
Who did his work and hadn't much to say,
And always laughed at other people's jokes
Because he hadn't any of his own.

That night when he was busy at his job
Of piling bags along the parapet,
He thought how slow time went, stamping his feet
And blowing on his fingers, pinched with cold.
He thought of getting back by half-past twelve,
And tot of rum to send him warm to sleep
In draughty dug-out frowsty with the fumes
Of coke, and full of snoring weary men.

He pushed another bag along the top,
Craning his body outward; then a flare
Gave one white glimpse of No Man's Land and wire;
And as he dropped his head the instant split
His startled life with lead, and all went out.

The Death-Bed

He drowsed and was aware of silence heaped
Round him, unshaken as the steadfast walls;
Aqueous like floating rays of amber light,
Soaring and quivering in the wings of sleep.
Silence and safety; and his mortal shore
Lipped by the inward, moonless waves of death.

Someone was holding water to his mouth.
He swallowed, unresisting; moaned and dropped
Through crimson gloom to darkness; and forgot
The opiate throb and ache that was his wound.
    Water – calm, sliding green above the weir.
    Water – a sky-lit alley for his boat,
    Bird-voiced, and bordered with reflected flowers
    And shaken hues of summer; drifting down,
    He dipped contented oars, and sighed, and slept.

Night, with a gust of wind, was in the ward,
Blowing the curtain to a glimmering curve.
Night. He was blind; he could not see the stars
Glinting among the wraiths of wandering cloud;
Queer blots of colour, purple, scarlet, green,
Flickered and faded in his drowning eyes.

Rain – he could hear it rustling through the dark;
Fragrance and passionless music woven as one;
Warm rain on drooping roses; pattering showers
That soak the woods; not the harsh rain that sweeps

Behind the thunder, but a trickling peace,
Gently and slowly washing life away.

He stirred, shifting his body; then the pain
Leapt like a prowling beast, and gripped and tore
His groping dreams with grinding claws and fangs.
    But someone was beside him; soon he lay
    Shuddering because that evil thing had passed.
    And death, who'd stepped toward him, paused and stared.

Light many lamps and gather round his bed.
Lend him your eyes, warm blood, and will to live.
Speak to him; rouse him; you may save him yet.
He's young; he hated War; how should he die
When cruel old campaigners win safe through?

But death replied: 'I choose him.' So he went,
And there was silence in the summer night;
Silence and safety; and the veils of sleep.
Then, far away, the thudding of the guns.

'They'

The Bishop tells us: 'When the boys come back
They will not be the same; for they'll have fought
In a just cause: they lead the last attack
On Anti-Christ; their comrades' blood has bought
New right to breed an honourable race,
They have challenged Death and dared him face to face.'

'We're none of us the same!' the boys reply.
'For George lost both his legs; and Bill's stone blind;
Poor Jim's shot through the lungs and like to die;
And Bert's gone syphilitic: you'll not find
A chap who's served that hasn't found *some* change.'
And the Bishop said: 'The ways of God are strange!'

'Blighters'

The House is crammed: tier beyond tier they grin
And cackle at the Show, while prancing ranks
Of harlots shrill the chorus, drunk with din;
'We're sure the Kaiser loves our dear old Tanks!'

I'd like to see a Tank come down the stalls,
Lurching to ragtime tunes, or 'Home, sweet Home',
And there'd be no more jokes in Music-halls
To mock the riddled corpses round Bapaume.

Base Details

If I were fierce and bald, and short of breath,
    I'd live with scarlet Majors at the Base,
And speed glum heroes up the line to death.
    You'd see me with my puffy petulant face,
Guzzling and gulping in the best hotel,
    Reading the Roll of Honour. 'Poor young chap,'
I'd say – 'I used to know his father well;
    Yes, we've lost heavily in this last scrap.'
And when the war is done and youth stone dead,
I'd toddle safely home and die – in bed.

The Rear-Guard

(Hindenburg Line, April 1917)

Groping along the tunnel, step by step,
He winked his prying torch with patching glare
From side to side, and sniffed the unwholesome air.

Tins, boxes, bottles, shapes too vague to know;
A mirror smashed, the mattress from a bed;
And he, exploring fifty feet below
The rosy gloom of battle overhead.

Tripping, he grabbed the wall; saw some one lie
Humped at his feet, half-hidden by a rug,
And stooped to give the sleeper's arm a tug.
'I'm looking for headquarters.' No reply.
'God blast your neck!' (For days he'd had no sleep)
'Get up and guide me through this stinking place.'
Savage, he kicked a soft unanswering heap,
And flashed his beam across the livid face
Terribly glaring up, whose eyes yet wore
Agony dying hard ten days before;
And fists of fingers clutched a blackening wound.

Alone he staggered on until he found
Dawn's ghost that filtered down a shafted stair
To the dazed, muttering creatures underground
Who hear the boom of shells in muffled sound.

At last, with sweat of horror in his hair,
He climbed through darkness to the twilight air,
Unloading hell behind him step by step.

The General

'Good-morning, good-morning!' the General said
When we met him last week on our way to the line.
Now the soldiers he smiled at are most of 'em dead,
And we're cursing his staff for incompetent swine.
'He's a cheery old card,' grunted Harry to Jack
As they slogged up to Arras with rifle and pack.

But he did for them both by his plan of attack.

Attack

At dawn the ridge emerges massed and dun
In wild purple of the glow'ring sun,
Smouldering through spouts of drifting smoke that shroud
The menacing scarred slope; and, one by one,
Tanks creep and topple forward to the wire.
The barrage roars and lifts. Then, clumsily bowed
With bombs and guns and shovels and battle-gear,
Men jostle and climb to meet the bristling fire.
Lines of grey, muttering faces, masked with fear,
They leave their trenches, going over the top,
While time ticks blank and busy on their wrists,
And hope, with furtive eyes and grappling fists,
Flounders in mud. O Jesus, make it stop!

Prelude: The Troops

Dim, gradual thinning of the shapeless gloom
Shudders to drizzling daybreak that reveals
Disconsolate men who stamp their sodden boots
And turn dulled, sunken faces to the sky
Haggard and hopeless. They, who have beaten down
The stale despair of night, must now renew
Their desolation in the truce of dawn,
Murdering the livid hours that grope for peace.

Yet these who cling to life with stubborn hands,
Can grin through storms of death and find a gap
In the clawed, cruel tangles of his defence.
They march from safety, and the bird-sung joy
Of grass-green thickets, to the land where all
Is ruin, and nothing blossoms but the sky
That hastens over them where they endure
Sad, smoking, flat horizons, reeking woods,
And foundered trench-lines volleying doom for doom.

O my brave brown companions, when your souls
Flock silently away, and the eyeless dead
Shame the wild beast of battle on the ridge,
Death will stand grieving in that field of war
Since your unvanquished hardihood is spent.
And through some mooned Valhalla there will pass
Battalions and battalions, scarred from hell;
The unreturning army that was youth;
The legions who have suffered and are dust.

Counter-Attack

We'd gained our first objective hours before
While dawn broke like a face with blinking eyes,
Pallid, unshaved and thirsty, blind with smoke.
Things seemed all right at first. We held their line,
With bombers posted, Lewis guns well placed,
And clink of shovels deepening the shallow trench.
   The place was rotten with dead; green clumsy legs
   High-booted, sprawled and grovelled along the saps
   And trunks, face downward, in the sucking mud,
   Wallowed like trodden sand-bags loosely filled;
   And naked sodden buttocks, mats of hair,
   Bulged, clotted heads slept in the plastering slime.
   And then the rain began, – the jolly old rain!

A yawning soldier knelt against the bank,
Staring across the morning blear with fog;
He wondered when the Allemands would get busy;
And then, of course, they started with five-nines
Traversing, sure as fate, and never a dud.
Mute in the clamour of shells he watched them burst
Spouting dark earth and wire with gusts from hell,
While posturing giants dissolved in drifts of smoke.
He crouched and flinched, dizzy with galloping fear,
Sick for escape, – loathing the strangled horror
And butchered, frantic gestures of the dead.

An officer came blundering down the trench:
'Stand-to and man the fire-step!' On he went . . .
Gasping and bawling, 'Fire-step . . . counter-attack!'
Then the haze lifted. Bombing on the right
Down the old sap: machine-guns on the left;
And stumbling figures looming out in front.
'O Christ, they're coming at us!' Bullets spat,
And he remembered his rifle . . . rapid fire . . .
And started blazing wildly . . . then a bang
Crumpled and spun him sideways, knocked him out
To grunt and wriggle: none heeded him; he choked
And fought the flapping veils of smothering gloom,
Lost in a blurred confusion of yells and groans . . .
Down, and down, and down, he sank and drowned,
Bleeding to death. The counter-attack had failed.

Everyone Sang

Everyone suddenly burst out singing;
And I was filled with such delight
As prisoned birds must find in freedom,
Winging wildly across the white
Orchards and dark-green fields; on – on – and out of sight.

Everyone's voice was suddenly lifted;
And beauty came like the setting sun:
My heart was shaken with tears; and horror
Drifted away ... O, but Everyone
Was a bird; and the song was wordless; the singing will
    never be done.

Anthem for Doomed Youth

What passing-bells for these who die as cattle?
   – Only the monstrous anger of the guns.
   Only the stuttering rifles' rapid rattle
Can patter out their hasty orisons.
No mockeries now for them; no prayers nor bells;
   Nor any voice of mourning save the choirs, –
The shrill, demented choirs of wailing shells;
   And bugles calling for them from sad shires.

What candles may be held to speed them all?
   Not in the hands of boys but in their eyes
Shall shine the holy glimmers of goodbyes.
   The pallor of girls' brows shall be their pall;
Their flowers the tenderness of patient minds,
And each slow dusk a drawing-down of blinds.

'I saw his round mouth's crimson . . .'

I saw his round mouth's crimson deepen as it fell,
 Like a sun, in his last deep hour;
Watched the magnificent recession of farewell,
 Clouding, half gleam, half glower,
And a last splendour burn the heavens of his cheek.
 And in his eyes
The cold stars lighting, very old and bleak,
 In different skies.

Dulce Et Decorum Est

Bent double, like old beggars under sacks,
Knock-kneed, coughing like hags, we cursed through sludge,
Till on the haunting flares we turned our backs
And towards our distant rest began to trudge.
Men marched asleep. Many had lost their boots
But limped on, blood-shod. All went lame; all blind;
Drunk with fatigue; deaf even to the hoots
Of tired, outstripped Five-Nines that dropped behind.

Gas! Gas! Quick, boys! – An ecstasy of fumbling,
Fitting the clumsy helmets just in time;
But someone still was yelling out and stumbling,
And flound'ring like a man in fire or lime . . .
Dim, through the misty panes and thick green light,
As under a green sea, I saw him drowning.

In all my dreams, before my helpless sight,
He plunges at me, guttering, choking, drowning.

If in some smothering dreams you too could pace
Behind the wagon that we flung him in,
And watch the white eyes writhing in his face,
His hanging face, like a devil's sick of sin;
If you could hear, at every jolt, the blood
Come gargling from the froth-corrupted lungs,
Obscene as cancer, bitter as the cud
Of vile, incurable sores on innocent tongues, –
My friend, you would not tell with such high zest

To children ardent for some desperate glory,
The old Lie: Dulce et decorum est
Pro patria mori.

The Dead-Beat

He dropped, – more sullenly than wearily,
Lay stupid like a cod, heavy like meat,
And none of us could kick him to his feet;
– Just blinked at my revolver, blearily;
– Didn't appear to know a war was on,
Or see the blasted trench at which he stared.
'I'll do 'em in,' he whined. 'If this hand's spared,
I'll murder them, I will.'

                A low voice said,
'It's Blighty, p'raps, he sees; his pluck's all gone,
Dreaming of all the valiant, that *aren't* dead:
Bold uncles, smiling ministerially;
Maybe his brave young wife, getting her fun
In some new home, improved materially.
It's not these stiffs have crazed him; nor the Hun.'

We sent him down at last, out of the way.
Unwounded; – stout lad, too, before that strafe.
Malingering? Stretcher-bearers winked, 'Not half!'

Next day I heard the Doc's well-whiskied laugh:
'That scum you sent last night soon died. Hooray!'

Strange Meeting

It seemed that out of battle I escaped
Down some profound dull tunnel, long since scooped
Through granites which titanic wars had groined.

Yet also there encumbered sleepers groaned,
Too fast in thought or death to be bestirred.
Then, as I probed them, one sprang up, and stared
With piteous recognition in fixed eyes,
Lifting distressful hands, as if to bless.
And by his smile, I knew that sullen hall, –
By his dead smile I knew we stood in Hell.

With a thousand pains that vision's face was grained;
Yet no blood reached there from the upper ground,
And no guns thumped, or down the flues made moan.
'Strange friend,' I said, 'here is no cause to mourn.'
'None,' said that other, 'save the undone years,
The hopelessness. Whatever hope is yours,
Was my life also; I went hunting wild
After the wildest beauty in the world,
Which lies not calm in eyes, or braided hair,
But mocks the steady running of the hour,
And if it grieves, grieves richlier than here.
For by my glee might many men have laughed,
And of my weeping something had been left,
Which must die now. I mean the truth untold,
The pity of war, the pity war distilled.
Now men will go content with what we spoiled,

Or, discontent, boil bloody, and be spilled.
They will be swift with swiftness of the tigress.
None will break ranks, though nations trek from progress.
Courage was mine, and I had mystery,
Wisdom was mine, and I had mastery:
To miss the march of this retreating world
Into vain citadels that are not walled.
Then, when much blood had clogged their chariot-wheels,
I would go up and wash them from sweet wells,
Even with truths that lie too deep for taint.
I would have poured my spirit without stint
But not through wounds; not on the cess of war.
Foreheads of men have bled where no wounds were.

'I am the enemy you killed, my friend.
I knew you in this dark: for so you frowned
Yesterday through me as you jabbed and killed.
I parried; but my hands were loath and cold.
Let us sleep now . . .'

Futility

Move him into the sun –
Gently its touch awoke him once,
At home, whispering of fields half-sown.
Always it woke him, even in France,
Until this morning and this snow.
If anything might rouse him now
The kind old sun will know.

Think how it wakes the seeds –
Woke once the clays of a cold star.
Are limbs, so dear achieved, are sides
Full-nerved, still warm, too hard to stir?
Was it for this the clay grew tall?
– O what made fatuous sunbeams toil
To break earth's sleep at all?

Mental Cases

Who are these? Why sit they here in twilight?
Wherefore rock they, purgatorial shadows,
Drooping tongues from jaws that slob their relish,
Baring teeth that leer like skulls' teeth wicked?
Stroke on stroke of pain, – but what slow panic,
Gouged these chasms round their fretted sockets?
Ever from their hair and through their hands' palms
Misery swelters. Surely we have perished
Sleeping, and walk hell; but who these hellish?

– These are men whose minds the Dead have ravished.
Memory fingers in their hair of murders,
Multitudinous murders they once witnessed.
Wading sloughs of flesh these helpless wander,
Treading blood from lungs that had loved laughter.
Always they must see these things and hear them,
Batter of guns and shatter of flying muscles,
Carnage incomparable, and human squander
Rucked too thick for these men's extrication.

Therefore still their eyeballs shrink tormented
Back into their brains, because on their sense
Sunlight seems a blood-smear; night comes blood-black;
Dawn breaks open like a wound that bleeds afresh.
– Thus their heads wear this hilarious, hideous,
Awful falseness of set-smiling corpses.
– Thus their hands are plucking at each other;

Picking at the rope-knouts of their scourging;
Snatching after us who smote them, brother,
Pawing us who dealt them war and madness.

The Send-Off

Down the close darkening lanes they sang their way
To the siding-shed,
And lined the train with faces grimly gay.

Their breasts were stuck all white with wreath and spray
As men's are, dead.

Dull porters watched them, and a casual tramp
Stood staring hard,
Sorry to miss them from the upland camp.

Then, unmoved, signals nodded, and a lamp
Winked to the guard.

So secretly, like wrongs hushed-up, they went.
They were not ours:
We never heard to which front these were sent;

Nor there if they yet mock what women meant
Who gave them flowers.

Shall they return to beating of great bells
In wild train-loads?
A few, a few, too few for drums and yells,

May creep back, silent, to village wells,
Up half-known roads.

Disabled

He sat in a wheeled chair, waiting for dark,
And shivered in his ghastly suit of grey,
Legless, sewn short at elbow. Through the park
Voices of boys rang saddening like a hymn,
Voices of play and pleasure after day,
Till gathering sleep had mothered them from him.

*

About this time Town used to swing so gay
When glow-lamps budded in the light blue trees,
And girls glanced lovelier as the air grew dim, –
In the old times, before he threw away his knees.
Now he will never feel again how slim
Girls' waists are, or how warm their subtle hands.
All of them touch him like some queer disease.

*

There was an artist silly for his face,
For it was younger than his youth, last year.
Now, he is old; his back will never brace;
He's lost his colour very far from here,
Poured it down shell-holes till the veins ran dry,
And half his lifetime lapsed in the hot race
And leap of purple spurted from his thigh.

*

One time he liked a blood-smear down his leg,
After the matches, carried shoulder-high.
It was after football, when he'd drunk a peg,

He thought he'd better join. – He wonders why.
Someone had said he'd look a god in kilts,
That's why; and maybe, too, to please his Meg,
Aye, that was it, to please the giddy jilts
He asked to join. He didn't have to beg;
Smiling they wrote his lie: aged nineteen years.

*

Germans he scarcely thought of; all their guilt,
And Austria's, did not move him. And no fears
Of Fear came yet. He thought of jewelled hilts
For daggers in plaid socks; of smart salutes;
And care of arms; and leave; and pay arrears;
Esprit de corps; and hints for young recruits.
And soon, he was drafted out with drums and cheers.

*

Some cheered him home, but not as crowds cheer Goal.
Only a solemn man who brought him fruits
Thanked him; and then enquired about his soul.

*

Now, he will spend a few sick years in institutes,
And do what things the rules consider wise,
And take whatever pity they may dole.
Tonight he noticed how the women's eyes
Passed from him to the strong men that were whole.
How cold and late it is! Why don't they come
And put him into bed? Why don't they come?

A Terre

(being the philosophy of many soldiers)

Sit on the bed. I'm blind, and three parts shell.
Be careful; can't shake hands now; never shall.
Both arms have mutinied against me, – brutes.
My fingers fidget like ten idle brats.

I tried to peg out soldierly, – no use!
One dies of war like any old disease.
This bandage feels like pennies on my eyes.
I have my medals? – Discs to make eyes close.
My glorious ribbons? – Ripped from my own back
In scarlet shreds. (That's for your poetry book.)

A short life and a merry one, my buck!
We used to say we'd hate to live dead-old, –
Yet now ... I'd willingly be puffy, bald,
And patriotic. Buffers catch from boys
At least the jokes hurled at them. I suppose
Little I'd ever teach a son, but hitting,
Shooting, war, hunting, all the arts of hurting.
Well, that's what I learnt, – that, and making money.

Your fifty years ahead seem none too many?
Tell me how long I've got? God! For one year
To help myself to nothing more than air!
One Spring! Is one too good to spare, too long?
Spring wind would work its own way to my lung,
And grow me legs as quick as lilac-shoots.

My servant's lamed, but listen how he shouts!
When I'm lugged out, he'll still be good for that.
Here in this mummy-case, you know, I've thought
How well I might have swept his floors for ever.
I'd ask no nights off when the bustle's over,
Enjoying so the dirt. Who's prejudiced
Against a grimed hand when his own's quite dust,
Less live than specks that in the sun-shafts turn,
Less warm than dust that mixes with arms' tan?

I'd love to be a sweep, now, black as Town,
Yes, or a muckman. Must I be his load?

O Life, Life, let me breathe, – a dug-out rat!
Not worse than ours the lives rats lead –
Nosing along at night down some safe rut,
They find a shell-proof home before they rot.
Dead men may envy living mites in cheese,
Or good germs even. Microbes have their joys,
And subdivide, and never come to death.
Certainly flowers have the easiest time on earth.
'I shall be one with nature, herb, and stone,'
Shelley would tell me. Shelley would be stunned:
The dullest Tommy hugs that fancy now.
'Pushing up daisies' is their creed, you know.

To grain, then, go my fat, to buds my sap,
For all the usefulness there is in soap.
D'you think the Boche will ever stew man-soup?
Some day, no doubt, if . . .
                                        Friend, be very sure
I shall be better off with plants that share
More peaceably the meadow and the shower.

Soft rains will touch me, – as they could touch once,
And nothing but the sun shall make me ware.
Your guns may crash around me. I'll not hear;
Or, if I wince, I shall not know I wince.

Don't take my soul's poor comfort for your jest.
Soldiers may grow a soul when turned to fronds,
But here the thing's best left at home with friends.

My soul's a little grief, grappling your chest,
To climb your throat on sobs; easily chased
On other sighs and wiped by fresher winds.

Carry my crying spirit till it's weaned
To do without what blood remained these wounds.

Exposure

Our brains ache, in the merciless iced east winds that knive
    us...
Wearied we keep awake because the night is silent...
Low, drooping flares confuse our memory of the salient...
Worried by silence, sentries whisper, curious, nervous,
        But nothing happens.

Watching, we hear the mad gusts tugging on the wire,
Like twitching agonies of men among its brambles.
Northward, incessantly, the flickering gunnery rumbles,
Far off, like a dull rumour of some other war.
        What are we doing here?

The poignant misery of dawn begins to grow...
We only know war lasts, rain soaks, and clouds sag stormy.
Dawn massing in the east her melancholy army
Attacks once more in ranks on shivering ranks of grey,
        But nothing happens.

Sudden successive flights of bullets streak the silence.
Less deathly than the air that shudders black with snow,
With sidelong flowing flakes that flock, pause, and renew;
We watch them wandering up and down the wind's
    nonchalance,
        But nothing happens.

Pale flakes with fingering stealth come feeling for our faces –
We cringe in holes, back on forgotten dreams, and stare,
　　snow-dazed,
Deep into grassier ditches. So we drowse, sun-dozed,
Littered with blossoms trickling where the blackbird fusses,
　　　　– Is it that we are dying?

Slowly our ghosts drag home: glimpsing the sunk fires, glozed
With crusted dark-red jewels; crickets jingle there;
For hours the innocent mice rejoice: the house is theirs;
Shutters and doors, all closed: on us the doors are closed, –
　　　　We turn back to our dying.

Since we believe not otherwise can kind fires burn;
Nor ever suns smile true on child, or field, or fruit.
For God's invincible spring our love is made afraid;
Therefore, not loath, we lie out here; therefore were born,
　　　　For love of God seems dying.

Tonight, this frost will fasten on this mud and us,
Shrivelling many hands, puckering foreheads crisp.
The burying-party, picks and shovels in shaking grasp,
Pause over half-known faces. All their eyes are ice,
　　　　But nothing happens.

The Sentry

We'd found an old Boche dug-out, and he knew,
And gave us hell; for shell on frantic shell
Lit full on top, but never quite burst through.
Rain, guttering down in waterfalls of slime,
Kept slush waist-high and rising hour by hour,
And choked the steps too thick with clay to climb.
What murk of air remained stank old, and sour
With fumes from whizz-bangs, and the smell of men
Who'd lived there years, and left their curse in the den,
If not their corpses . . .
                              There we herded from the blast
Of whizz-bangs; but one found our door at last, –
Buffeting eyes and breath, snuffing the candles,
And thud! flump! thud! down the steep steps came thumping
And sploshing in the flood, deluging muck, –
The sentry's body; then his rifle, handles
Of old Boche bombs, and mud in ruck on ruck.
We dredged it up, for dead, until he whined,
'O sir – my eyes, – I'm blind, – I'm blind, – I'm blind.'
Coaxing, I held a flame against his lids
And said if he could see the least blurred light
He was not blind; in time they'd get all right.
'I can't,' he sobbed. Eyeballs, huge-bulged like squids',
Watch my dreams still, – yet I forgot him there
In posting Next for duty, and sending a scout
To beg a stretcher somewhere, and flound'ring about
To other posts under the shrieking air.

Those other wretches, how they bled and spewed,
And one who would have drowned himself for good, –
I try not to remember these things now.
Let Dread hark back for one word only: how,
Half-listening to that sentry's moans and jumps,
And the wild chattering of his shivered teeth,
Renewed most horribly whenever crumps
Pummelled the roof and slogged the air beneath, –
Through the dense din, I say, we heard him shout
'I see your lights!' – But ours had long gone out.

Spring Offensive

Halted against the shade of a last hill
They fed, and eased of pack-loads, were at ease;
And leaning on the nearest chest or knees
Carelessly slept.
              But many there stood still
To face the stark blank sky beyond the ridge,
Knowing their feet had come to the end of the world.
Marvelling they stood, and watched the long grass swirled
By the May breeze, murmurous with wasp and midge;
And though the summer oozed into their veins
Like an injected drug for their bodies' pains,
Sharp on their souls hung the imminent ridge of grass,
Fearfully flashed the sky's mysterious glass.

Hour after hour they ponder the warm field
And the far valley behind, where buttercups
Had blessed with gold their slow boots coming up;
When even the little brambles would not yield
But clutched and clung to them like sorrowing arms.
They breathe like trees unstirred.

Till like a cold gust thrills the little word
At which each body and its soul begird
And tighten them for battle. No alarms
Of bugles, no high flags, no clamorous haste, –
Only a lift and flare of eyes that faced
The sun, like a friend with whom their love is done.

O larger shone that smile against the sun, –
Mightier than his whose bounty these have spurned.

So, soon they topped the hill, and raced together
Over an open stretch of herb and heather
Exposed. And instantly the whole sky burned
With fury against them; earth set sudden cups
In thousands for their blood; and the green slope
Chasmed and deepened sheer to infinite space.

Of them who running on that last high place
Breasted the surf of bullets, or went up
On the hot blast and fury of hell's upsurge,
Or plunged and fell away past this world's verge,
Some say God caught them even before they fell.

But what say such as from existence' brink
Ventured but drave too swift to sink,
The few who rushed in the body to enter hell,
And there out-fiending all its fiends and flames
With superhuman inhumanities,
Long-famous glories, immemorial shames –
And crawling slowly back, have by degrees
Regained cool peaceful air in wonder –
Why speak not they of comrades that went under?

Field Ambulance in Retreat
Via Dolorosa, Via Sacra

I

A straight flagged road, laid on the rough earth,
A causeway of stone from beautiful city to city,
Between the tall trees, the slender, delicate trees,
Through the flat green land, by plots of flowers, by black
  canals thick with heat.

II

The road-makers made it well
Of fine stone, strong for the feet of the oxen and of the great
  Flemish horses,
And for the high wagons piled with corn from the harvest.
And the labourers are few;
They and their quiet oxen stand aside and wait
By the long road loud with the passing of the guns, the rush of
  armoured cars, and the tramp of an army on the march
  forward to battle;
And, where the piled corn-wagons went, our dripping
  Ambulance carries home
Its red and white harvest from the fields.

III

The straight flagged road breaks into dust, into a thin white
  cloud,
About the feet of a regiment driven back league by league,
Rifles at trail, and standards wrapped in black funeral cloths.
Unhasting, proud in retreat,

[124]

They smile as the Red Cross Ambulance rushes by.
(You know nothing of beauty and of desolation who have
 not seen
That smile of an army in retreat.)
They go: and our shining, beckoning danger goes with them,
And our joy in the harvests that we gathered in at nightfall in
 the fields;
And like an unloved hand laid on a beating heart
Our safety weighs us down.

Safety hard and strange; stranger and yet more hard
As, league after dying league, the beautiful, desolate Land
Falls back from the intolerable speed of an Ambulance in
 retreat
On the sacred, dolorous Way.

Gethsemane

The Garden called Gethsemane
    In Picardy it was,
And there the people came to see
    The English soldiers pass.
We used to pass – we used to pass
    Or halt, as it might be,
And ship our masks in case of gas
    Beyond Gethsemane.

The Garden called Gethsemane,
    It held a pretty lass,
But all the time she talked to me
    I prayed my cup might pass.
The officer sat on the chair,
    The men lay on the grass,
And all the time we halted there
    I prayed my cup might pass.

It didn't pass – it didn't pass –
    It didn't pass from me.
I drank it when we met the gas
    Beyond Gethsemane!

My Boy Jack

'Have you news of my boy Jack?'
   Not this tide.
'When d'you think that he'll come back?'
   Not with this wind blowing, and this tide.

'Has any one else had word of him?'
   Not this tide.
For what is sunk will hardly swim,
   Not with this wind blowing, and this tide.

'Oh, dear, what comfort can I find?'
   None this tide,
   Nor any tide,
Except he did not shame his kind –
   Not even with that wind blowing, and that tide.

Then hold your head up all the more,
   This tide,
   And every tide;
Because he was the son you bore,
   And gave to that wind blowing and that tide!

Epitaphs of the War

'Equality of Sacrifice'

A. 'I was a Have.' B. 'I was a "have-not."'
  (*Together*.) 'What hast thou given which I gave not?'

A Servant

We were together since the War began.
He was my servant – and the better man.

A Son

My son was killed while laughing at some jest. I would I knew
What it was, and it might serve me in a time when jests are few.

An Only Son

I have slain none except my Mother. She
(Blessing her slayer) died of grief for me.

Ex-clerk

Pity not! The Army gave
Freedom to a timid slave:
In which Freedom did he find
Strength of body, will, and mind:
By which strength he came to prove
Mirth, Companionship, and Love:
For which Love to Death he went:
In which Death he lies content.

The Wonder

Body and Spirit I surrendered whole
To harsh Instructors – and received a soul . . .
If mortal man could change me through and through
From all I was – what may The God not do?

Hindu Sepoy in France

This man in his own country prayed we know not to what
  Powers.
We pray Them to reward him for his bravery in ours.

The Coward

I could not look on Death, which being known,
Men led me to him, blindfold and alone.

Shock

My name, my speech, my self I had forgot.
My wife and children came – I knew them not.
I died. My Mother followed. At her call
And on her bosom I remembered all.

A Grave near Cairo

Gods of the Nile, should this stout fellow here
Get out – get out! He knows not shame nor fear.

Pelicans in the Wilderness
A Grave near Halfa

The blown sand heaps on me, that none may learn
  Where I am laid for whom my children grieve . . .
O wings that beat at dawning, ye return
  Out of the desert to your young at eve!

Two Canadian Memorials

I

We giving all gained all.
　　Neither lament us nor praise.
Only in all things recall,
　　It is Fear, not Death that slays.

II

From little towns in a far land we came,
　　To save our honour and a world aflame.
By little towns in a far land we sleep;
　　And trust that world we won for you to keep!

The Favour

Death favoured me from the first, well knowing I could not
　　endure
To wait on him day by day. He quitted my betters and came
Whistling over the fields, and, when he had made all sure,
　　'Thy line is at end,' he said, 'but at least I have saved its name.'

The Beginner

On the first hour of my first day
　　In the front trench I fell.
(Children in boxes at a play
　　Stand up to watch it well.)

R.A.F. (Aged Eighteen)

Laughing through clouds, his milk-teeth still unshed,
Cities and men he smote from overhead.
His deaths delivered, he returned to play
Childlike, with childish things now put away.

The Refined Man

I was of delicate mind. I stepped aside for my needs,
　　Disdaining the common office. I was seen from afar and
　　　　killed . . .
How is this matter for mirth? Let each man be judged by his
　　deeds
　　I have paid my price to live with myself on the terms that I willed.

Native Water-Carrier (M.E.F.)

Prometheus brought down fire to men.
　　This brought up water.
The Gods are jealous – now, as then,
　　Giving no quarter.

Bombed in London

On land and sea I strove with anxious care
To escape conscription. It was in the air!

The Sleepy Sentinel

Faithless the watch that I kept: now I have none to keep.
I was slain because I slept: now I am slain I sleep.
Let no man reproach me again, whatever watch is unkept –
I sleep because I am slain. They slew me because I slept.

Batteries out of Ammunition

If any mourn us in the workshop, say
We died because the shift kept holiday.

Common Form

If any question why we died,
Tell them, because our fathers lied.

A Dead Statesman

I could not dig: I dared not rob:
Therefore I lied to please the mob.
Now all my lies are proved untrue
And I must face the men I slew.
What tale shall serve me here among
Mine angry and defrauded young?

The Rebel

If I had clamoured at Thy Gate
    For gift of Life on Earth,
And, thrusting through the souls that wait,
    Flung headlong into birth –
Even then, even then, for gin and snare
    About my pathway spread,
Lord, I had mocked Thy thoughtful care
    Before I joined the Dead!
But now? . . . I was beneath Thy Hand
    Ere yet the Planets came.
And now – though Planets pass, I stand
    The witness to Thy shame!

The Obedient

Daily, though no ears attended,
    Did my prayers arise.
Daily, though no fire descended,
    Did I sacrifice.
Though my darkness did not lift,
    Though I faced no lighter odds,
Though the Gods bestowed no gift,
                None the less,
    None the less, I served the Gods!

A Drifter off Tarentum

He from the wind-bitten North with ship and companions
    descended,
  Searching for eggs of death spawned by invisible hulls.
Many he found and drew forth. Of a sudden the fishery ended
  In flame and a clamorous breath known to the eye-pecking
    gulls.

Destroyers in Collision

For Fog and Fate no charm is found
  To lighten, or amend.
I, hurrying to my bride, was drowned –
  Cut down by my best friend.

Convoy Escort

I was a shepherd to fools
  Causelessly bold or afraid.
They would not abide by my rules.
  Yet they escaped. For I stayed.

Unknown Female Corpse

Headless, lacking foot and hand,
Horrible I come to land.
I beseech all women's sons
Know I was a mother once.

Raped and Revenged

One used and butchered me: another spied
Me broken – for which thing an hundred died.
So it was learned among the heathen hosts
How much a freeborn woman's favour costs.

[133]

Salonikan Grave

I have watched a thousand days
Push out and crawl into night
Slowly as tortoises.
Now I, too, follow these.
It is fever, and not the fight –
Time, not battle, – that slays.

The Bridegroom

Call me not false, beloved,
   If, from thy scarce-known breast
So little time removed,
   In other arms I rest.

For this more ancient bride,
   Whom coldly I embrace,
Was constant at my side
   Before I saw thy face.

Our marriage, often set –
   By miracle delayed –
At last is consummate,
   And cannot be unmade.

Live, then, whom Life shall cure,
   Almost, of Memory,
And leave us to endure
   Its immortality.

V.A.D. *(Mediterranean)*

Ah, would swift ships had never been, for then we ne'er had
  found,
These harsh Ægean rocks between, this little virgin drowned,
Whom neither spouse nor child shall mourn, but men she
  nursed through pain
And – certain keels for whose return the heathen look in vain.

Actors

On a Memorial Tablet in Holy Trinity Church, Stratford-on-Avon

We counterfeited once for your disport
    Men's joy and sorrow: but our day has passed.
We pray you pardon all where we fell short –
    Seeing we were your servants to this last.

Journalists

On a Panel in the Hall of the Institute of Journalists

We have served our day.

The Cenotaph
September 1919

Not yet will those measureless fields be green again
Where only yesterday the wild sweet blood of wonderful
     youth was shed;
There is a grave whose earth must hold too long, too deep a
     stain,
Though for ever over it we may speak as proudly as we may
     tread.
But here, where the watchers by lonely hearths from the thrust
     of an inward sword have more slowly bled,
We shall build the Cenotaph: Victory, winged, with Peace,
     winged too, at the column's head.
And over the stairway, at the foot – oh! here, leave desolate,
     passionate hands to spread
Violets, roses, and laurel, with the small, sweet, twinkling
     country things
Speaking so wistfully of other Springs,
From the little gardens of little places where son or sweetheart
     was born and bred.
In splendid sleep, with a thousand brothers
                    To lovers – to mothers
                    Here, too, lies he:
Under the purple, the green, the red,
It is all young life: it must break some women's hearts to see
Such a brave, gay coverlet to such a bed!
Only, when all is done and said,
God is not mocked and neither are the dead.

For this will stand in our Market-place –
                    Who'll sell, who'll buy
                    (Will you or I
Lie each to each with the better grace)?
While looking into every busy whore's and huckster's face
As they drive their bargains, is the Face
Of God: and some young, piteous, murdered face.

from *Hugh Selwyn Mauberley*
(Life and contacts)

These fought in any case,
and some believing,
.   pro domo, in any case . . .

Some quick to arm,
some for adventure,
some from fear of weakness,
some from fear of censure,
some for love of slaughter in imagination,
learning later . . .
some in fear, learning love of slaughter;
Died some, pro patria,
non 'dulce' non 'et decor' . . .
walked eye-deep in hell
believing in old men's lies, then unbelieving
came home, home to a lie,
home to many deceits,
home to old lies and new infamy;
usury age-old and age-thick
and liars in public places.

Daring as never before, wastage as never before.
Young blood and high blood,
fair cheeks, and fine bodies;

fortitude as never before

frankness as never before,
disillusions as never told in the old days,
hysterias, trench confessions,
laughter out of dead bellies.

*

There died a myriad,
And of the best, among them,
For an old bitch gone in the teeth,
For a botched civilization,

Charm, smiling at the good mouth,
Quick eyes gone under earth's lid,

For two gross of broken statues,
For a few thousand battered books.

Triumphal March

Stone, bronze, stone, steel, stone, oakleaves, horses' heels
Over the paving.
And the flags. And the trumpets. And so many eagles.
How many? Count them. And such a press of people.
We hardly knew ourselves that day, or knew the City.
This is the way to the temple, and we so many crowding the
    way.
So many waiting, how many waiting? what did it matter, on
    such a day?
Are they coming? No, not yet. You can see some eagles.
    And hear the trumpets.
Here they come. Is he coming?
The natural wakeful life of our Ego is a perceiving.
We can wait with our stools and our sausages.
What comes first? Can you see? Tell us. It is

    5,800,000 rifles and carbines,
       102,000 machine guns,
        28,000 trench mortars,
        53,000 field and heavy guns,
I cannot tell how many projectiles, mines and fuses,
        13,000 aeroplanes,
        24,000 aeroplane engines,
        50,000 ammunition waggons,
now 55,000 army waggons,
       11,000 field kitchens,
        1,150 field bakeries.

What a time that took. Will it be he now? No,
Those are the golf club Captains, these the Scouts,
And now the *société gymnastique de Poissy*
And now come the Mayor and the Liverymen. Look
There he is now, look:
There is no interrogation in his eyes
Or in the hands, quiet over the horse's neck,
And the eyes watchful, waiting, perceiving, indifferent.
O hidden under the dove's wing, hidden in the turtle's breast,
Under the palmtree at noon, under the running water
At the still point of the turning world. O hidden.

Now they go up to the temple. Then the sacrifice.
Now come the virgins bearing urns, urns containing
Dust
Dust
Dust of dust, and now
Stone, bronze, stone, steel, stone, oakleaves, horses' heels
Over the paving.

That is all we could see. But how many eagles! and how many
        trumpets!
(And Easter Day, we didn't get to the country,
So we took young Cyril to church. And they rang a bell
And he said right out loud, *crumpets*.)
                        Don't throw away that sausage,
It'll come in handy. He's artful. Please, will you
Give us a light?
Light
Light
Et les soldats faisaient la haie? ILS LA FAISAIENT.

HUGH MCDIARMID

Another Epitaph on an Army of Mercenaries

It is a God-damned lie to say that these
Saved, or knew, anything worth any man's pride.
They were professional murderers, and they took
    Their blood money, and impious risks, and died.
In spite of all their kind, some elements of worth
    Persist with difficulty here and there on earth.

MCMXIV

Those long uneven lines
Standing as patiently
As if they were stretched outside
The Oval or Villa Park,
The crowns of hats, the sun
On moustached archaic faces
Grinning as if it were all
An August Bank Holiday lark;

And the shut shops, the bleached
Established names on the sunblinds,
The farthings and sovereigns,
And dark-clothed children at play
Called after kings and queens,
The tin advertisements
For cocoa and twist, and the pubs
Wide open all day –

And the countryside not caring:
The place names all hazed over
With flowering grasses, and fields
Shadowing Domesday lines
Under wheat's restless silence;

The differently-dressed servants
With tiny rooms in huge houses,
The dust behind limousines;

Never such innocence,
Never before or since,
As changed itself to past
Without a word – the men
Leaving the gardens tidy,
The thousands of marriages,
Lasting a little while longer:
Never such innocence again.

D. J. ENRIGHT

A Grand Night

When the film *Tell England* came
To Leamington, my father said,
'That's about Gallipoli – I was there.
I'll call and see the manager . . .'

Before the first showing, the manager
Announced that 'a local resident . . .' etc.
And there was my father on the stage
With a message to the troops from Sir Somebody
Exhorting, condoling or congratulating.
But he was shy, so the manager
Read it out, while he fidgeted.
Then the lights went off, and I thought
I'd lost my father.
The Expedition's casualty rate was 50%.

But it was a grand night,
With free tickets for the two of us.

The Great War

Whenever war is spoken of
I find
The war that was called Great invades the mind:
The grey militia marches over land
A darker mood of grey
Where fractured tree-trunks stand
And shells, exploding, open sudden fans
Of smoke and earth.
Blind murders scythe
The deathscape where the iron brambles writhe;
The sky at night
Is honoured with rosettes of fire,
Flares that define the corpses on the wire
As terror ticks on wrists at zero hour.
These things I see,
But they are only part
Of what it is that slyly probes the heart:
Less vivid images and words excite
The sensuous memory
And, even as I write,
Fear and a kind of love collaborate
To call each simple conscript up
For quick inspection:
Trenches' parapets
Paunchy with sandbags; bandoliers, tin-hats.
Candles in dug-outs,
Duckboards, mud and rats.
Then, like patrols, tunes creep into the mind:

A long, long trail, The Rose of No-Man's Land,
Home Fire and *Tipperary*:
And through the misty keening of a band
Of Scottish pipes the proper names are heard
Like fateful commentary of distant guns:
Passchendaele, Bapaume, and Loos, and Mons.
And now,
Whenever the November sky
Quivers with a bugle's hoarse, sweet cry,
The reason darkens; in its evening gleam
Crosses and flares, tormented wire, grey earth
Splattered with crimson flowers,
And I remember,
Not the war I fought in
But the one called Great
Which ended in a sepia November
Four years before my birth.

Six Young Men

The celluloid of a photograph holds them well –
Six young men, familiar to their friends.
Four decades that have faded and ochre-tinged
This photograph have not wrinkled the faces or the hands.
Though their cocked hats are not now fashionable,
Their shoes shine. One imparts an intimate smile,
One chews a grass, one lowers his eyes, bashful,
One is ridiculous with cocky pride –
Six months after this picture they all were dead.

All are trimmed for a Sunday jaunt. I know
That bilberried bank, that thick tree, that black wall,
Which are there yet and not changed. From where these sit
You hear the water of seven streams fall
To the roarer in the bottom, and through all
The leafy valley a rumouring of air go.
Pictured here, their expressions listen yet,
And still that valley has not changed in sound
Though their faces are four decades under the ground.

This one was shot in an attack and lay
Calling in the wire, then this one, his best friend,
Went out to bring him in and was shot too;
And this one, the very moment he was warned
From potting at tin-cans in no-man's land,
Fell back dead with his rifle-sights shot away.
The rest, nobody knows what they came to,

But come to the worst they must have done, and held it
Closer than their hope; all were killed.

Here, see a man's photograph,
The locket of a smile, turned overnight
Into the hospital of his mangled last
Agony and hours; see bundled in it
His mightier-than-man dead bulk and weight:
And on this one place which keeps him alive
(In his Sunday best) see fall war's worst
Thinkable flash and rending, onto his smile
Forty years rotting into soil.

That man's not more alive whom you confront
And shake by the hand, see hale, hear speak loud,
Than any of these six celluloid smiles are,
Nor prehistoric or fabulous beast more dead;
No thought so vivid as their smoking blood:
To regard this photograph might well dement,
Such contradictory permanent horrors here
Smile from the single exposure and shoulder out
One's own body from its instant and heat.

TED HUGHES

The Last of the 1st/5th Lancashire Fusiliers
A Souvenir of the Gallipoli Landings

The father capers across the yard cobbles
Look, like a bird, a water-bird, an ibis going over pebbles
We laughed, like warships fluttering bunting.

Heavy-duty design, deep-seated in ocean-water
The warships flutter bunting.
A fiesta day for the warships
Where war is only an idea, as drowning is only an idea
In the folding of a wave, in the mourning
Funeral procession, the broadening wake
That follows a ship under power.

War is an idea in the muzzled calibre of the big guns.
In the grey, wolvish outline.
War is a kind of careless health, like the heart-beat
In the easy bodies of sailors, feeling the big engines
Idling between emergencies.

It is what has left the father
Who has become a bird.
Once he held war in his strong pint mugful of tea
And drank at it, heavily sugared.
It was all for him
Under the parapet, under the periscope, the look-out
Under Achi Baba and the fifty billion flies.

Now he has become a long-billed, spider-kneed bird
Bow-backed, finding his footing, over the frosty cobbles
A wader, picking curiosities from the shallows.

His sons don't know why they laughed, watching him through
    the window
Remembering it, remembering their laughter
They only want to weep
  As after the huge wars

  Senseless huge wars

  Huge senseless weeping.

SEAMUS HEANEY

Veteran's Dream

Mr Dickson, my neighbour,
Who saw the last cavalry charge
Of the war and got the first gas
Walks with a limp

Into his helmet and khaki.
He notices indifferently
The gas has yellowed his buttons
And near his head

Horses plant their shods.
His real fear is gangrene.
He wakes with his hand to the scar
And they do their white magic

Where he lies
On cankered ground,
A scatter of maggots, busy
In the trench of his wound.

Wounds

Here are two pictures from my father's head –
I have kept them like secrets until now:
First, the Ulster Division at the Somme
Going over the top with 'Fuck the Pope!'
'No Surrender!': a boy about to die,
Screaming 'Give 'em one for the Shankill!'
'Wilder than Gurkhas' were my father's words
Of admiration and bewilderment.
Next comes the London-Scottish padre
Resettling kilts with his swagger-stick,
With a stylish backhand and a prayer.
Over a landscape of dead buttocks
My father followed him for fifty years.
At last, a belated casualty,
He said – lead traces flaring till they hurt –
'I am dying for King and Country, slowly.'
I touched his hand, his thin head I touched.

Now, with military honours of a kind,
With his badges, his medals like rainbows,
His spinning compass, I bury beside him
Three teenage soldiers, bellies full of
Bullets and Irish beer, their flies undone.
A packet of Woodbines I throw in,
A lucifer, the Sacred Heart of Jesus
Paralysed as heavy guns put out
The night-light in a nursery for ever;
Also a bus-conductor's uniform –

He collapsed beside his carpet-slippers
Without a murmur, shot through the head
By a shivering boy who wandered in
Before they could turn the television down
Or tidy away the supper dishes.
To the children, to a bewildered wife,
I think 'Sorry Missus' was what he said.

MICHAEL LONGLEY

The War Poets

Unmarked were the bodies of the soldier-poets
For shrapnel opened up again the fontanel
Like a hailstone melting towards deep water
At the bottom of a well, or a mosquito
Balancing its tiny shadow above the lip.

It was rushes of air that took the breath away
As though curtains were drawn suddenly aside
And darkness streamed into the dormitory
Where everybody talked about the war ending
And always it would be the last week of the war.

In Memoriam

My father, let no similes eclipse
Where crosses like some forest simplified
Sink roots into my mind; the slow sands
Of your history delay till through your eyes
I read you like a book. Before you died,
Re-enlisting with all the broken soldiers
You bent beneath your rucksack, near collapse,
In anecdote rehearsed and summarised
These words I write in memory. Let yours
And other heartbreaks play into my hands.

Now I see in close-up, in my mind's eye,
The cracked and splintered dead for pity's sake
Each dismal evening predecease the sun,
You, looking death and nightmare in the face
With your kilt, harmonica and gun,
Grow older in a flash, but none the wiser
(Who, following the wrong queue at The Palace,
Have joined the London Scottish by mistake),
Your nineteen years uncertain if and why
Belgium put the kibosh on the Kaiser.

Between the corpses and the soup canteens
You swooned away, watching your future spill.
But, as it was, your proper funeral urn
Had mercifully smashed to smithereens
To shrapnel shards that sliced your testicle.
That instant I, your most unlikely son,

In No Man's Land was surely left for dead,
Blotted out from your far horizon.
As your voice now is locked inside my head,
I yet was held secure, waiting my turn.

Finally, that lousy war was over.
Stranded in France and in need of proof
You hunted down experimental lovers,
Persuading chorus girls and countesses:
This, father, the last confidence you spoke.
In my twentieth year your old wounds woke
As cancer. Lodging under the same roof
Death was a visitor who hung about,
Strewing the house with pills and bandages,
Till he chose to put your spirit out.

Though they overslept the sequence of events
Which ended with the ambulance outside,
You lingering in the hall, your bowels on fire,
Tears in your eyes, and all your medals spent,
I summon girls who packed at last and went
Underground with you. Their souls again on hire,
Now those lost wives as recreated brides
Take shape before me, materialise
On the verge of light and happy legend
They lift their skirts like blinds across your eyes.

Truce

It begins with one or two soldiers
And one or two following
With hampers over their shoulders.
They might be off wildfowling

As they would another Christmas Day,
So gingerly they pick their steps.
No one seems sure of what to do.
All stop when one stops.

A fire gets lit. Some spread
Their greatcoats on the frozen ground.
Polish vodka, fruit and bread
Are broken out and passed round.

The air of an old German song,
The rules of Patience, are the secrets
They'll share before long.
They draw on their last cigarettes

As Friday-night lovers, when it's over,
Might get up from their mattresses
To congratulate each other
And exchange names and addresses.

My Grandfather at the Pool
i.m. James Maxwell 1895–1980

This photo I know best of him is him
With pals of his about to take a swim,

Forming a line with four of them, so five
All told one afternoon, about to dive:

Merseysiders, grinning and wire-thin,
Still balanced, not too late to not go in,

Or feint to but then teeter on a whim.
The only one who turned away is him,

About to live the trenches and survive,
Alone, as luck would have it, of the five.

Four gazing at us levelly, one not.
Another pal decided on this shot,

Looked down into the box and said *I say*
And only James looked up and then away.

I narrow my own eyes until they blur.
In a blue sneeze of a cornfield near Flers

In 1969, he went *Near here*

It happened and he didn't say it twice.
It's summer and the pool will be like ice.

Five pals in Liverpool about to swim.
The only one who looks away is him.

The other four look steadily across
The water and the joke they share to us.

Wholly and coldly gone, they meet our eyes
Like stars the eye is told are there and tries

To see – all pity flashes back from there,
Till I too am the unnamed unaware

And things are stacked ahead of me so vast
I sun myself in shadows that they cast:

Things I dreamed but never dreamed were there,
But are and may by now be everywhere,

When you're what turns the page or looks away.
When I'm what disappears into my day.

Acknowledgements

EDMUND BLUNDEN: 'Concert Party: Busseboom', 'Pillbox', 'Festubert, 1916' and ' "Transport Up" at Ypres' from *Selected Poems* (Carcanet Press, 1982), reprinted by permission of the Peters Fraser & Dunlop Group. MAY WEDDERBURN CANNAN: 'Rouen' from *In War Time* (Blackwell, 1917), reprinted by permission of James Slater. MARGARET POSTGATE COLE: 'The Veteran' and 'Praematuri' from *An Anthology of War Poems*, edited by Frederick Brereton (William Collins, 1930), reprinted by permission of David Higham Associates. T. S. ELIOT: 'Triumphal March' from *Collected Poems 1909–1962* (Faber and Faber, 1974), reprinted by permission of the publisher. D. J. ENRIGHT: 'A Grand Night' from *Collected Poems 1948–1998* (Oxford Poets, 1998/Carcanet Press), reprinted by permission of Watson, Little Ltd (Authors' Agents). ELEANOR FARJEON: 'Easter Monday' from *First and Second Love* (Oxford University Press, 1959), reprinted by permission of David Higham Associates. WILFRID GIBSON: 'Breakfast', 'Mark Anderson' and 'A Lament' from *Collected Poems 1906–1925* (Macmillan, 1926), reprinted by permission of Macmillan, London. ROBERT GRAVES: 'The Legion' from *Collected Poems* (Cassell, 1975), reprinted by permission of Carcanet Press. IVOR GURNEY: 'Song', 'To His Love', 'First Time In', 'After War', 'The Silent One', 'Strange Hells', 'The Interview', 'The Mangel-Bury', 'The Bohemians', 'Varennes' and 'War Books' from *Collected Poems of Ivor Gurney*, edited by P. J. Kavanagh (Oxford University Press, 1982), reprinted by permission of The Ivor Gurney Trust. SEAMUS HEANEY: 'Veteran's Dream' from

Wintering Out (Faber and Faber, 1972), reprinted by permission of the publisher. A. E. HOUSMAN: 'Epitaph on an Army of Mercenaries' from *Collected Poems and Selected Prose* (Penguin Twentieth-Century Classics, 1989). TED HUGHES: 'Six Young Men' and 'The Last of the 1st/5th Lancashire Fusiliers' from *New Selected Poems 1957–1994* (Faber and Faber, 1995), reprinted by permission of the publisher. DAVID JONES: from Part 4 of *In Parenthesis* (Faber and Faber, 1937), reprinted by permission of the publisher. RUDYARD KIPLING: 'Gethsemane', 'My Boy Jack' and 'Epitaphs of the War' from *Rudyard Kipling: The Complete Verse* (Kyle Cathie Ltd, 1996). PHILIP LARKIN: 'MCMXIV' from *Collected Poems* (Faber and Faber, 1988), reprinted by permission of the publisher. MICHAEL LONGLEY: 'Wounds', 'The War Poets' and 'In Memoriam' from *Selected Poems* (Jonathan Cape, 1998), reprinted by permission of the Random House Group. ROSE MACAULAY: from 'Picnic' from *Three Days* (Constable & Co., 1919), reprinted by permission of the Peters Fraser & Dunlop Group. HUGH MACDIARMID: 'Another Epitaph on an Army of Mercenaries' from *MacDiarmid: Selected Poems* (Penguin Twentieth-Century Classics, 1994), reprinted by permission of Carcanet Press. HELEN MACKAY: 'Train', reprinted in *Minds at War: The Poetry and Experience of the First World War* by David Roberts (Saxon Books, 1996). GLYN MAXWELL: 'My Grandfather at the Pool' from *The Breakage* (Faber and Faber, 1998), reprinted by permission of the publisher. CHARLOTTE MEW: 'The Cenotaph' from *Collected Poems and Prose*, edited by Val Warner (Virago/Carcanet Press, 1982), reprinted by permission of Carcanet Press. PAUL MULDOON: 'Truce' from *New Selected Poems 1968–1994* (Faber and Faber, 1996), reprinted by permission of the publisher. EZRA POUND: from 'Hugh Selwyn Mauberley' from *Collected Shorter Poems* (Faber and Faber, 1984), reprinted by permission of the publisher.

HERBERT READ: from 'Kneeshaw Goes to War' from *Collected Poems* (Faber and Faber, 1946), reprinted by permission of David Higham Associates. EDGELL RICKWORD: 'Winter Warfare' from *Behind the Eyes: Collected Poems and Selected Translations* (Carcanet Press, 1976), reprinted by permission of the publisher. SIEGFRIED SASSOON: 'A Working Party', 'The Death-Bed', 'They', 'Blighters', 'Base Details', 'The Rear-Guard', 'The General', 'Attack', 'Prelude: The Troops', 'Counter-Attack' and 'Everyone Sang' from *Collected Poems 1908–1956* (Faber and Faber, 1984), reprinted by permission of Barbara Levy Literary Agency. VERNON SCANNELL: 'The Great War' from *Collected Poems: 1950–1993* (Robson Books, 1994), reprinted by permission of the author. MAY SINCLAIR: 'Field Ambulance in Retreat' from *King Albert's Book*, edited by Hall Caine (Hodder & Stoughton, 1914). W. B. YEATS: 'On Being Asked for a War Poem' and 'An Irish Airman Foresees His Death' from *Collected Poems* (Picador, 1990).

Every effort has been made to trace or contact all copyright holders. The publishers would be pleased to rectify any omissions brought to their notice at the earliest opportunity.

Index of Poets

Index of First Lines

It is a God-damned lie to say that these, 142
It seemed that out of battle I escaped, 107
It was after war; Edward Thomas had fallen at Arras, 76
Just see what's happening, Worley! – Worley rose, 40
Laughing through clouds, his milk-teeth still unshed, 130
Move him into the sun, 109
Mr Dickson, my neighbour, 152
My father, let no similes eclipse, 156
My name, my speech, my self I had forgot, 130
My son was killed while laughing at some jest. I wish I knew, 128
Not yet will those measureless fields be green again, 136
Nudes – stark and glistening, 81
On land and sea I strove with anxious care, 131
On the first hour of the first day, 130
On the low table by the bed, 48
One got peace of heart at last, the dark march over, 71
One used and butchered me: another spied, 133
Only a man harrowing clods, 7
Only the wanderer, 68
Our brains ache, in the merciless iced east winds that knive us, 118
Pity not! The Army gave, 128
Prometheus brought down fire to men, 131
Rain, midnight rain, nothing but the wild rain, 26
Saints have adored the lofty soul of you, 21
Sit on the bed. I'm blind, and three parts shell, 115
Sombre the night is, 82
Stone, bronze, stone, steel, stone, oakleaves, horses' heels, 140
Such, such is death: no triumph: no defeat, 21
That night your great guns, unawares, 3
The Bells of Hell go ting-a-ling-a-ling, 61
The Bishop tells us: 'When the boys come back', 91

[169]

The blown sand heaps on me, that none may learn, 129
The celluloid of a photograph holds them well, 148
The cherry trees bend over and are shedding, 30
The darkness crumbles away, 80
The father capers across the yard cobbles, 150
The flowers left thick at nightfall in the wood, 24
The Garden called Gethsemane, 126
The House is crammed: tier beyond tier they grin, 92
The naked earth is warm with spring, 12
The plunging limbers over the shattered track, 83
The stage was set, the house was packed, 38
The storeman found the complement correct, 54
The sun used to shine while we two walked, 31
The thoroughfares that seem so dead to daylight passers-by, 43
There are a few left who will find it hard to forget, 51
There are strange Hells within the minds War made, 73
These fought in any case, 138
These, in the day when heaven was falling, 60
This is no case of petty right or wrong, 25
This man in his own country prayed we know not to what Powers, 129
This photo I know best of him is him, 159
Those long uneven lines, 143
Three hours ago he blundered up the trench, 87
Tiddleywinks, old man, 64
Tired with dull grief, grown old before my day, 41
Unmarked were the bodies of the soldier-poets, 155
We ate our breakfast lying on our backs. 47
We came upon him sitting in the sun, 44
We counterfeited once for your disport, 135
We giving all gained all, 130
We have served our day, 135

We lay and ate sweet hurt-berries, 50
We'd found an old Boche dug-out, and he knew, 120
We'd gained our first objective hours before, 99
We who are left, how shall we look again, 49
We were together since the War began, 128
What did they expect of our toil and extreme, 79
What of the faith and fire within us, 5
What passing-bells for these who die as cattle, 102
When men are old, and their friends die, 45
When the film *Tell England* came, 145
When you see millions of the mouthless dead, 23
Whenever war is spoken of, 146
Who are these? Why sit they here in twilight, 110
Who died on the wires, and hung there, one of two, 72
Will the train never start, 9